Stationery Flight

Extraordinary
Paper Airplanes

*Introduction by
Florence Temko*

Michael Weinstein

Cypress House

D1365205

Stationery Flight
Extraordinary Paper Airplanes
Copyright ©2004 by Michael Weinstein

Cypress House
155 Cypress Street
Fort Bragg, CA 95437
(800) 773-7782
www.cypresshouse.com

Cover and book design: Michael Brechner / Cypress House
Cover background photo: Copyright © 1999
Rixanne Wehren / GeoGraphics

    Library of Congress Cataloging-in-Publication Data
Weinstein, Michael, 1962-
    Stationery flight : extraordinary paper airplanes / Michael Weinstein
        p. cm.
    Includes bibliographical references.
    ISBN 1-879384-46-9 (alk. paper)

    1. Paper airplanes. I. Title.
    TL778.W45 2003
    745.592--dc21   2003053053

Printed in the USA
2 4 6 8 9 7 5 3 1

Contents

Introduction

Prepare to immerse yourself in the world of flight and origami with *Stationery Flight.* This book contains directions for constructing unusual paper airplanes, using a wide variety of folding techniques. Michael Weinstein combines his extensive knowledge of origami with his interest in aerodynamics (he flies his own airplane) to create a collection of paper models that includes gliders, fighter jets, bombers, an antique biplane, and other craft. Some exhibit little resemblance to conventional airplanes, yet all are capable of flight. Along the way, Michael explains aerodynamic forces, and describes origami techniques that you'll enjoy immensely.

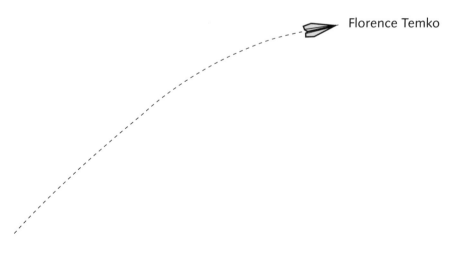 Florence Temko

Why Paper Airplanes Fly:

Because we throw them.

This is partly correct. Any object will fly if given sufficient thrust. Rockets are simply engines with fins, and even your grandfather's Buick will fly if you attach a large enough engine (indeed its flight characteristics may even surpass its road handling). Paper airplanes are no different. Rocks fly just fine, as do dishes, crystal, and various other common household items. On the other hand, flying rocks and other items are not a very efficient use of energy. Hurled with the same force, a well-made paper airplane suited to high-speed launch will fly much farther than a rock. And it takes more fuel for a missile to traverse the same distance as an airplane. The reason is that airplanes, both paper and real, generate their own upward force, called lift. All objects in flight have a number of forces acting on them, including thrust, drag, weight, and lift:

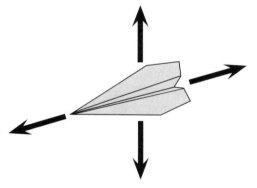

Lift: *An upward force generated by the wings.*

Drag: *The friction of the object with air. The smoother the object, the less friction and the less drag. That's one reason baseballs fly farther than rocks.*

Thrust: *The force that moves the object forward. In the case of rocks and paper airplanes, it's the acceleration of throwing them.*

Weight: *The Earth's gravity pulls any object toward the ground.*

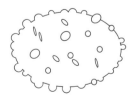

Rocks generate lift too, but very, very little. Baseballs actually generate lift in the direction of their spin, which is why a good pitcher can throw curve balls and sinkers.

So where does this lift stuff come from? Its existence comes from the fact that fluids (and gases, like air) exert less pressure when their velocity increases, as first described by an Italian named Bernoulli over two hundred years ago. To see how this affects airplanes, we need to examine an airplane's wing. The shape of a typical wing shows its curvature, or camber. The curve on the top of the wing, or airfoil, is what causes it to have lift. To see why, let's examine the travel of air across the wing.

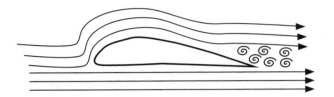 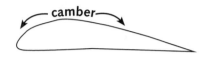

camber

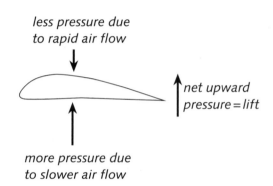

less pressure due
to rapid air flow

net upward
pressure = lift

more pressure due
to slower air flow

Notice that the air on the upper surface of the wing has to travel farther than the air on the bottom. Since it has to travel farther, the air on top speeds up. But remember Bernoulli? He discovered that when air speeds up, it exerts less pressure. Since the air on top exerts less pressure than the air on the bottom, there is a net upward force, or lift. All airplane wings exert lift, even paper ones. The little curlicues shown at the back of the wing represent turbulence, which is produced when air moves from regions of high to low velocity. This produces drag.

The more lift, the more drag. Airplanes have devices called flaps, which increase lift and drag, so that they can fly at lower speeds for landing. But now we run into a problem. Paper airplane wings are not curved, but are relatively flat. What gives?

To understand this, we have to talk about a long-deceased engineer named Osbourne Reynolds, who figured out how viscosity affects the behavior of liquids. Viscosity is an indication of the stickiness of a liquid or gas. Reynolds developed a formula to determine the effect of air on an object; thus every object has its own Reynolds number. For a paper airplane the number is in the tens of thousands, while it's in the millions for a real airplane. This means that from a paper airplane's perspective, air is very sticky. It is therefore hard for something tiny to produce lots of lift, but easy to make plenty of drag.

So paper airplanes have very thin wings, which produce less lift and less drag. Fortunately, paper is light, and little lift is needed to keep an average paper airplane aloft for the time it takes to traverse the living room. The effect of the Reynolds number can be seen in the shape of animal wings: bird wings are thick and shaped like an airfoil; bees have very flat wings, as they have lower Reynolds numbers and are governed by the viscosity of air. Real airplanes are so large that the camber of their wings is easily visible.

The length of the wing is referred to as its **chord**, while the distance across is its **span**. Wingspan divided by wing chord equals the **aspect ratio**, an important measure of how much drag a wing will produce. Swept-back wings have a low aspect ratio, and produce little drag. Rectangular, thick wings produce more. We can see how the shape of the wing affects the flight of a paper airplane with a couple of examples.

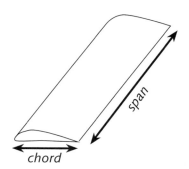

span / chord = Aspect Ratio

Example 1:

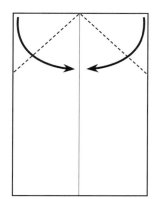 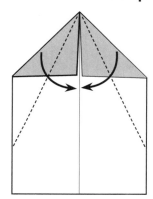 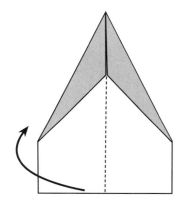 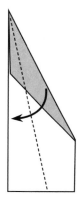

Mountain fold.

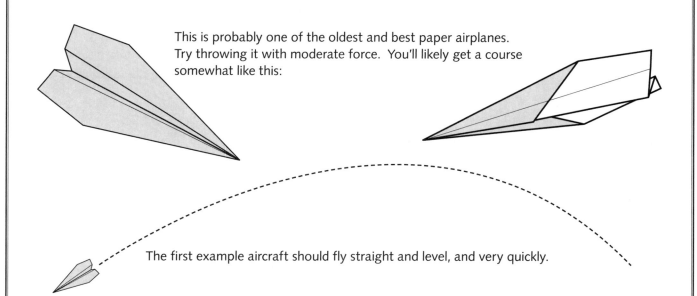

This is probably one of the oldest and best paper airplanes. Try throwing it with moderate force. You'll likely get a course somewhat like this:

The first example aircraft should fly straight and level, and very quickly.

Example 2:

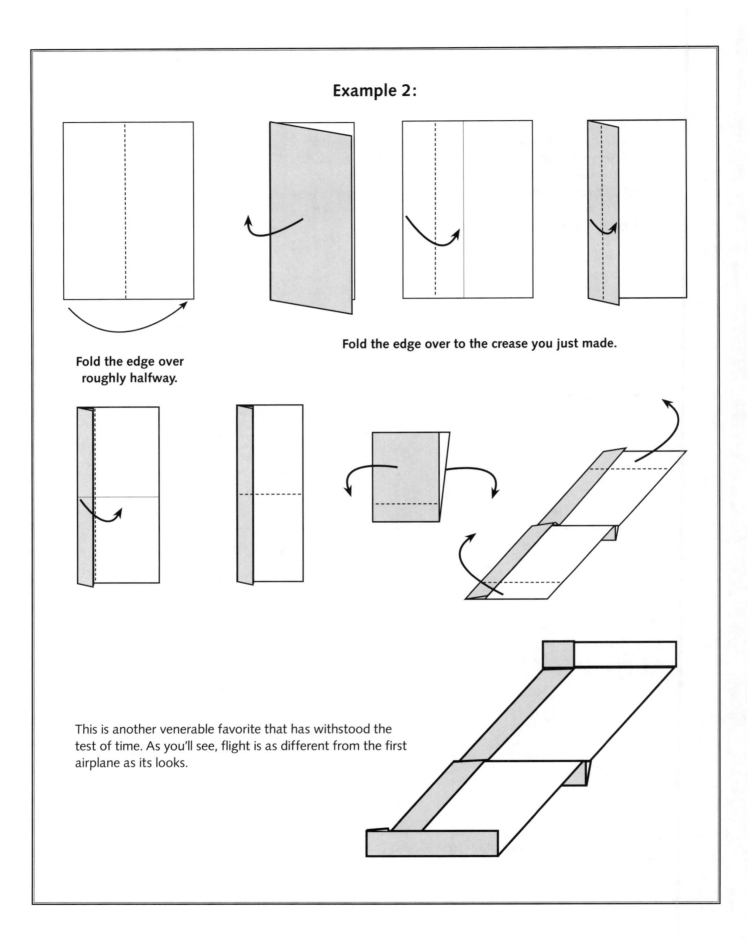

Fold the edge over
roughly halfway.

Fold the edge over to the crease you just made.

This is another venerable favorite that has withstood the test of time. As you'll see, flight is as different from the first airplane as its looks.

Try throwing this airplane as you did the first. See the difference? This airplane shoots up instead of flying straight and level. Since lift depends on thrust, you can try giving it a lighter throw to get less of an upward course. You'll notice that the airplane flies more slowly than the first. Why? There are some obvious differences between these two airplanes. For instance, one has swept-back wings, while the other has straight wings. How does that affect the aspect ratio?

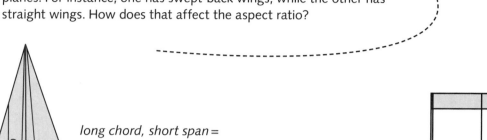

long chord, short span =
big aspect ratio

chord

span

short chord, long span =
small aspect ratio

In the first example, the wing chord is variable. But we can define an average wing chord by drawing one roughly through the middle of the wing.

Notice that the faster airplane has a longer chord and smaller span, which makes its aspect ratio much higher, and reduces drag. That's one reason why Example 2 flies so much more slowly. But Example 2 also shows much more lift than Example 1. Why? To answer that question we should look at a cross-section of the two wings:

Example 1   **Example 2**

The wing in Example 2 resembles an airfoil much more closely than Example 1. It therefore produces more lift and tends to nose up. It also produces more drag, so it slows down. This combination of factors affects many of the paper airplanes you will be folding, and can be used to get better, or more customized flight from an airplane. But there are other good ways to make the same airplane fly very different flight paths. A normal airplane has to ascend, descend, turn, and do many other things. Both paper and real airplanes use **trim** to fly the way their pilots want.

Trim

You can further control the flight of your airplane by using control surfaces and trim. Real airplanes have a number of these control surfaces, including elevators, ailerons, and rudder. The elevators control the pitch, or whether the airplane points up or down. That can be handy if you want to take off or land. The rudder turns the aircraft left or right, and is said (in pilot lingo) to control the yaw. The ailerons control whether the wings are level, or are canted at an angle. This is called **roll**, and the angle between the wings and the ground is called the **angle of bank**.

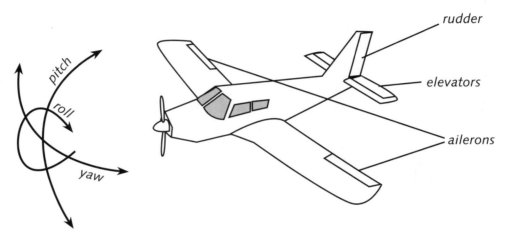

Paper airplanes also have control surfaces. This can be demonstrated by giving Example Airplane 1 elevators. Fold Example Airplane 1 and throw it. Notice how it flies. Now, fold small flaps up in the rear of the wings. These will act like the elevators in a real airplane. Notice how this affects the plane's performance.

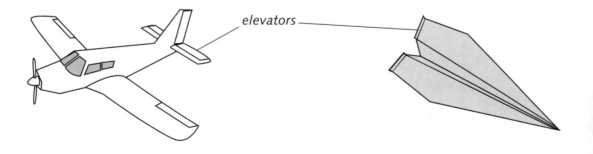

The elevator tends to force the tail end of the aircraft down and the nose up, causing it to fly a higher course. Of course, the elevators also increase drag, causing the plane to fly more slowly.

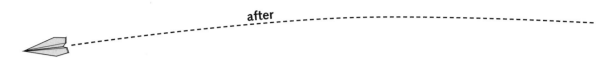

after

before

On a real airplane, the elevator can also be used to point the nose down for descent. You can do the same thing with a paper plane. Example Airplane 1 is not in need of any down elevator, but Example Airplane 2 could use some to straighten out its course. Fold Example Airplane 2, and give it some down elevator by making small flaps in the back and bending them down. This should bring the rear of the airplane up and the nose down, leveling off an otherwise unstable flight. Elevator can be used to give an airplane a smoother course, or to give its flight an upward or downward path, depending on what you like. The important thing is that it gives you a chance to decide how your airplane will fly.

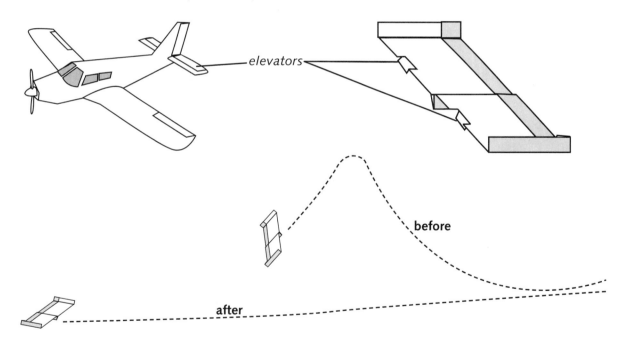

elevators

before

after

You can do more with trim than just level out an airplane's flight. Using horizontal and vertical control surfaces, you can make your airplane do almost anything you want.

The flaps on paper airplanes can also be used as ailerons, which bank real airplanes in order to turn them. Bicycles, motorcycles, and speedboats also bank in turns. To give your airplane ailerons, bend one flap up and the other down.

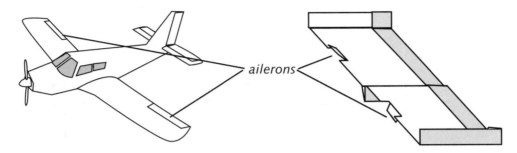

ailerons

Try giving this airplane a really gentle throw, and watch carefully. You'll see the wings start going at an angle, and the entire plane should turn to one side.

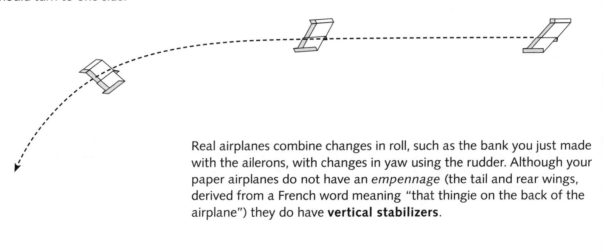

Real airplanes combine changes in roll, such as the bank you just made with the ailerons, with changes in yaw using the rudder. Although your paper airplanes do not have an *empennage* (the tail and rear wings, derived from a French word meaning "that thingie on the back of the airplane") they do have **vertical stabilizers**.

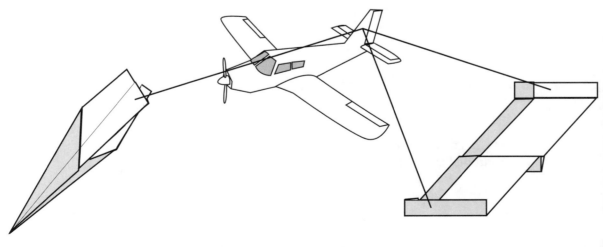

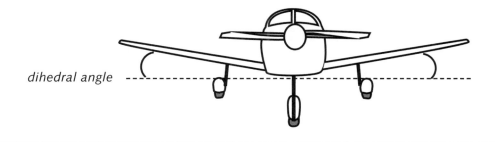

You can use the vertical stabilizers of your example airplanes for rudders to make them turn in flight. Try bending the vertical stabilizers of Example Airplane 2. It's a bit tricky, as the vertical stabilizers are attached to the wing, but it can be done. Now give the plane an easy toss. Notice how it adopts a turning flight, similar to what it did with the aileron adjustments? Now "for the cat's meow", combine the ailerons with the rudder. You can use these adjustments to get a number of different flight characteristics out of the same airplane! Example Airplane 2 is not the best airplane on which to use trim, as the vertical control surfaces are small, and the aspect ratio is extreme. Example Airplane 1 suffers similarly. But, there are lots of planes in *Stationery Flight* that have nice big control surfaces and intermediate aspect ratios, you can try all different kinds of trim!

Dihedral

The next time you're at your local airport, have a look at the airplanes, and look closely at the wings. You'll find that they're slightly upswept, like the Piper Cherokee shown. This wing angle, called *dihedral*, can stabilize an aircraft along its longitudinal axis, from front to back.

Normal airplanes have a limit to the amount of dihedral they can use, because if they have too much they go into what's known as a Dutch Roll, which involves really scary back-and-forth movements of the plane. The good thing is that paper airplanes don't Dutch Roll (or if they do it isn't scary, since you're on the ground), so you can use just as much dihedral as you like to stabilize an airplane in flight. Notice that dihedral is an upward angle.

Downward angle, or *anhedral*, is used in some really swoopy fighter jets, but it usually doesn't work very well in paper airplanes, although it works in a few of the highly unusual designs of *Stationery Flight*. Each airplane has a front view where the recommended dihedral and angles for vertical stabilizers are shown. However, every airplane is a bit different, so feel free to play with the trim and dihedral to make the plane do what you want.

dihedral angle

Symbols

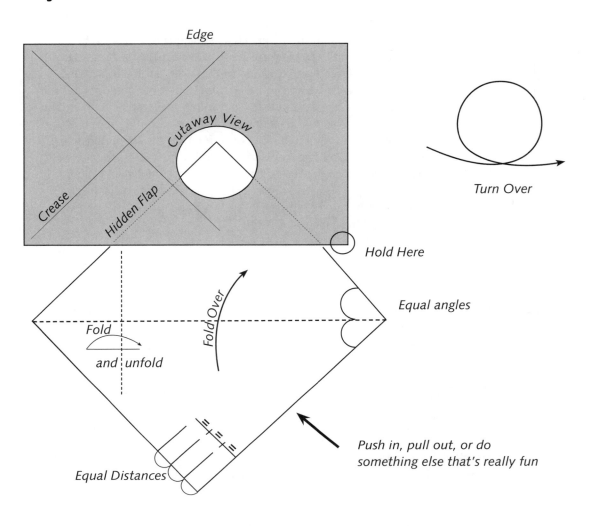

Edge

Cutaway View

Crease

Hidden Flap

Turn Over

Hold Here

Equal angles

Fold Over

Fold and unfold

Push in, pull out, or do something else that's really fun

Equal Distances

Valley fold

Fold so the crease points away from you (and the flap toward you).

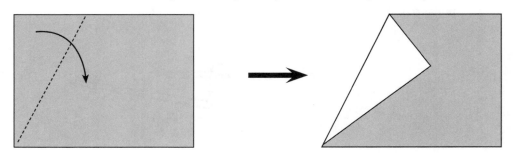

Mountain fold

Fold so that the crease points toward you
(and the flap away from you).

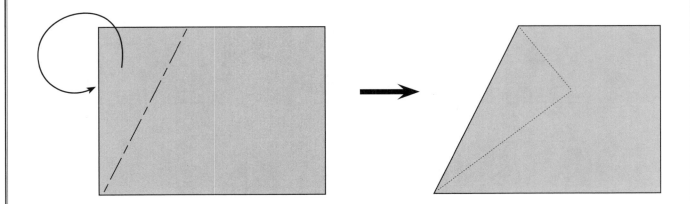

Inside Reverse fold

Fold so that a point falls between layers.

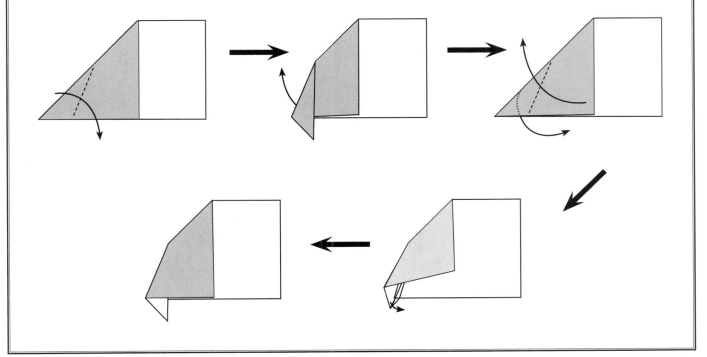

Outside Reverse fold

Fold so that a point wraps around the outside of two layers.

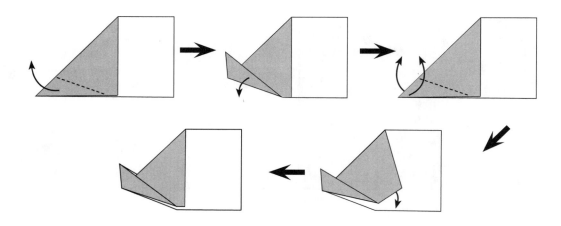

Rabbit Ear

Pull out a hidden layer and fold it flat.

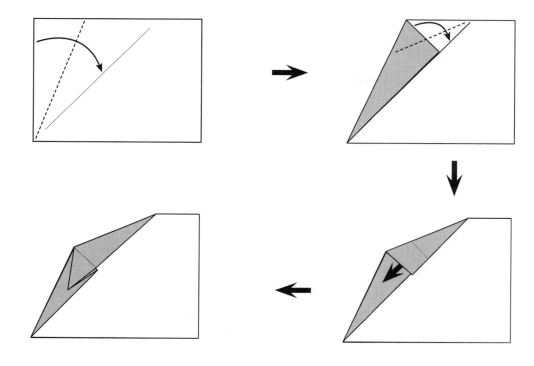

Squash fold

Separate two adjacent layers and flatten the pocket that forms between them.

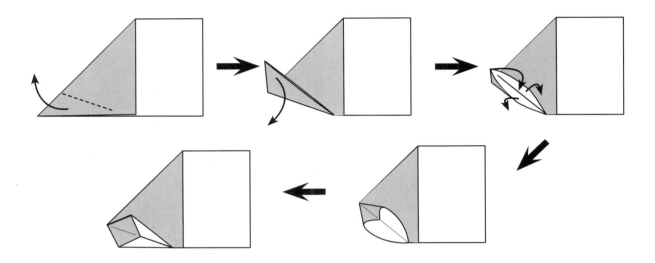

Petal fold

Separate two layers while flattening the pockets that form on either side.

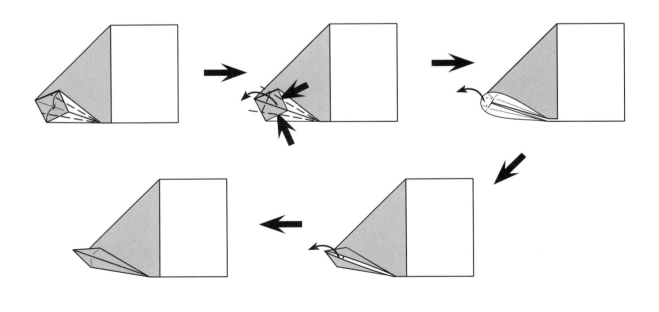

Sink fold

A multi-layered point gets pushed to the inside. The point is partially unfolded and mountain folded at the desired position.

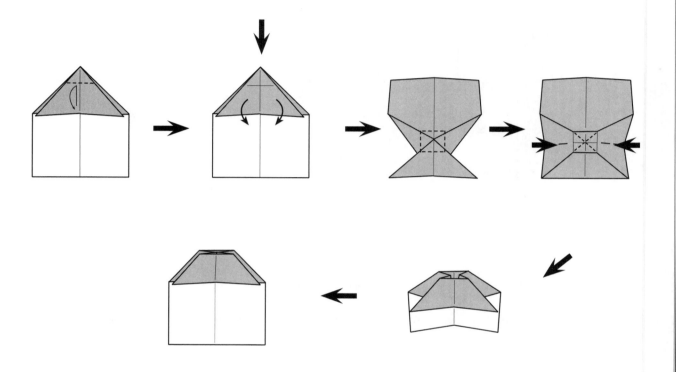

Paper Airplane Bases

Origami models often involve the same steps at the beginning. For example, if you wanted to fold a bird, you would need a head, neck, tail, and wings. In fact, one of the classic origami bases is the bird base, from which these structures are easily derived. The origami genius John Montrol has developed a dog base, from which one can readily fold the parts needed for a four-footed animal. Many of the airplanes in *Stationery Flight* are derived from a set of common precursors, instructions for which follow on the next page. The Airplane Base is short, and generates two evenly sized sets of wings. The Canard Base is the basis for most of the canard, or forward-wing aircraft.

Airplane Base

This will make two sets of wings, or one set of wings and one set of...

1.

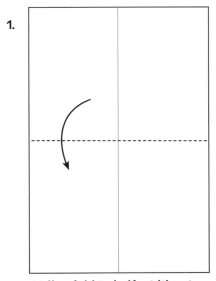

Valley fold in half width-wise.

2.

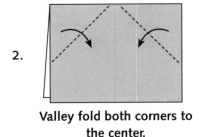

Valley fold both corners to the center.

3.

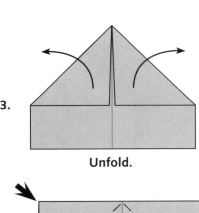

Unfold.

4.

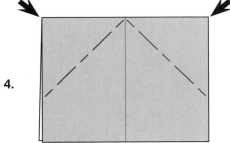

Reverse fold the corners inward.

5.

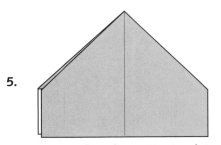

Paper airplane base #1 complete.

Canard Base

This base makes it easy to design canard, or forward-wing aircraft, because it generates two flaps in the front that can easily be manipulated to make many shapes and do a number of interesting things.

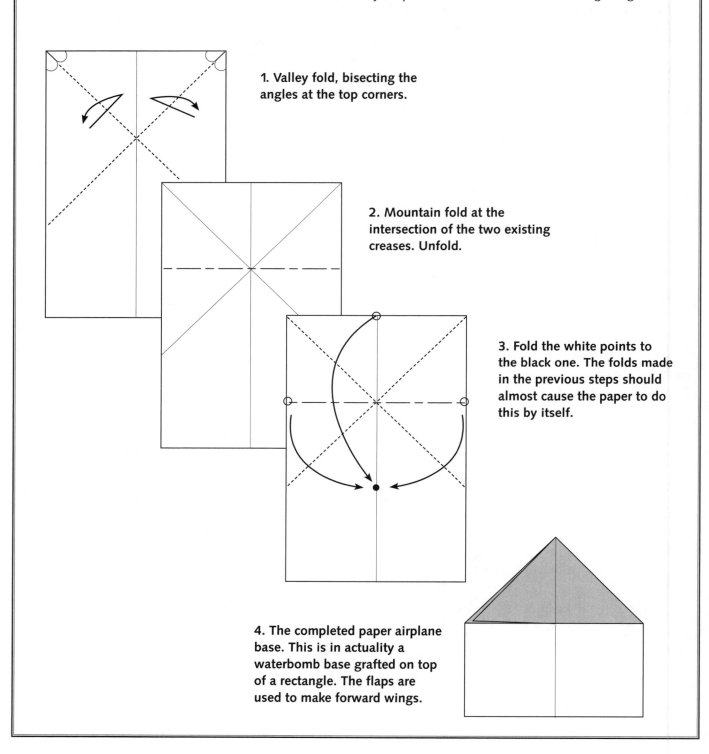

1. Valley fold, bisecting the angles at the top corners.

2. Mountain fold at the intersection of the two existing creases. Unfold.

3. Fold the white points to the black one. The folds made in the previous steps should almost cause the paper to do this by itself.

4. The completed paper airplane base. This is in actuality a waterbomb base grafted on top of a rectangle. The flaps are used to make forward wings.

Making and flying paper airplanes is educational, recreational, environmental (all that recycling of paper) and just plain fun. There are, of course, a few things that aid in the pursuit of the perfect plane.

Paper

Many kinds of paper are good for the aspiring parchment pilot. All of them are reasonably thick and strong; newspaper makes lousy fighter bombers, for instance. On the other hand, too much thickness spoils the party. Posterboard makes for really tough Origami, and most reasonably cool paper airplanes wouldn't dream of being made from construction paper. The paper must also hold a crease fairly well, so most softer papers are way out of it. Copier paper is one of my favorites, as it combines strength, light weight, and durability.

All but one of the *Stationery Flight* airplanes are made from paper that is 8½ × 5½ inches. This is not some mysterious paper only available in the finer bookstores of Tibet, but is a half sheet of ordinary 8½ × 11 inch paper, available everywhere. When creating my cellulose squadron I noticed that a normal-sized piece of paper was sort of short and didn't leave me much room to play around and do fun and interesting things (like use a Pagoda to create Canard wings). I found that a half-sheet was longer, and more fun to create with.

The craft contained within are all indoor flyers (growing up in northern Ohio, we had to appreciate good-weather days, all two of them). Being manufactured from smaller paper makes them lighter and more nimble than their larger brethren. Making the required size of paper is very simple; fold an 8½ × 11 piece of paper in half, and cut along the crease. A paper-cutter makes it even easier. If you're locked in a room with none of these things, you can simply tear a piece of paper in half.

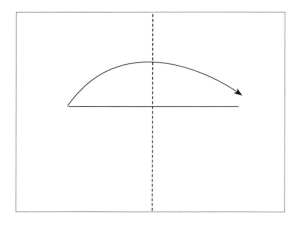

How to Make an 8½ × 5½ Inch Sheet of Paper

Fold an 8½ × 11 inch sheet of paper in half, and crease really well. Unfold.

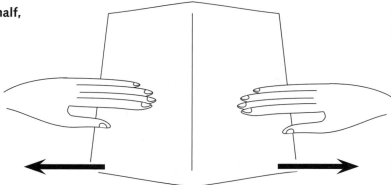

Hold the paper so the crease faces up toward you. Pull evenly around the crease at the part nearest to you.

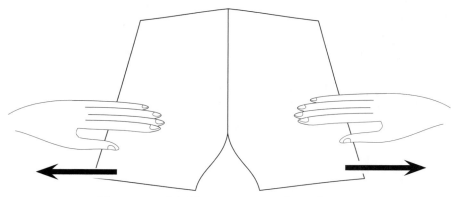

The paper should start to tear where the midline crease meets the forward edge. Continue to apply pressure evenly, and the paper will tear very neatly in half. With a bit of practice, this becomes really easy, and faster than scissors!

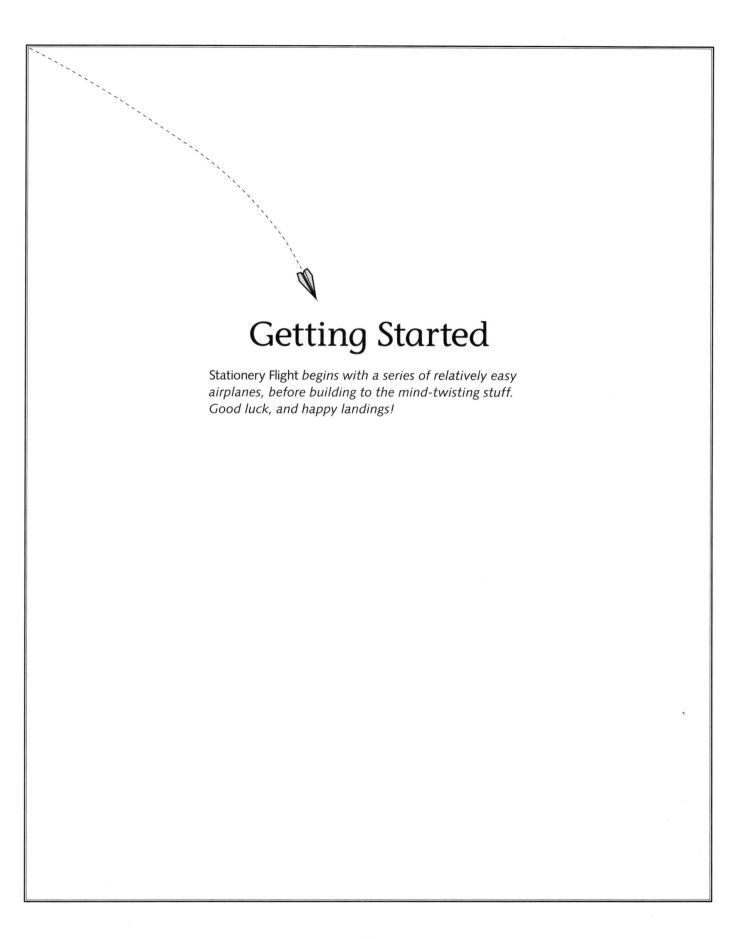

Getting Started

Stationery Flight *begins with a series of relatively easy airplanes, before building to the mind-twisting stuff. Good luck, and happy landings!*

Thirdsies

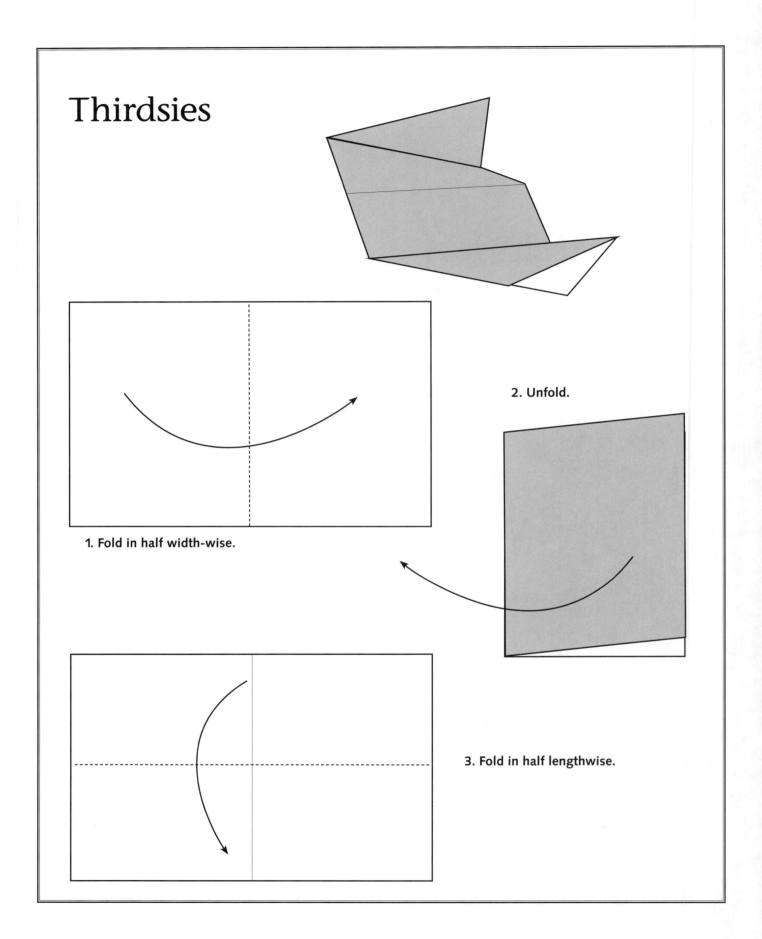

1. Fold in half width-wise.

2. Unfold.

3. Fold in half lengthwise.

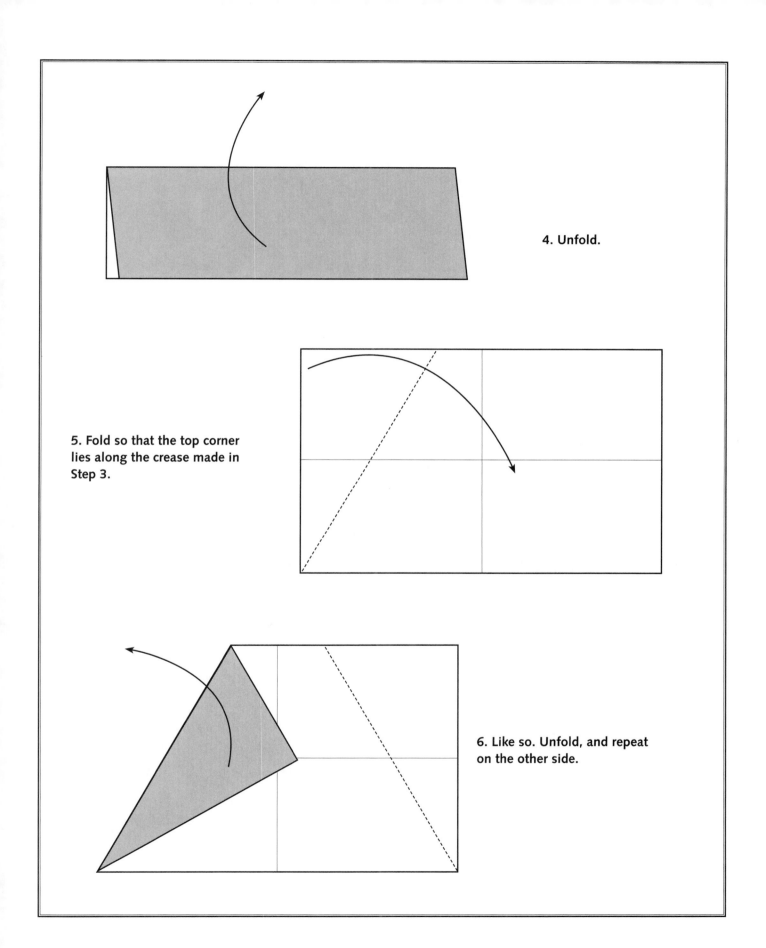

4. Unfold.

5. Fold so that the top corner lies along the crease made in Step 3.

6. Like so. Unfold, and repeat on the other side.

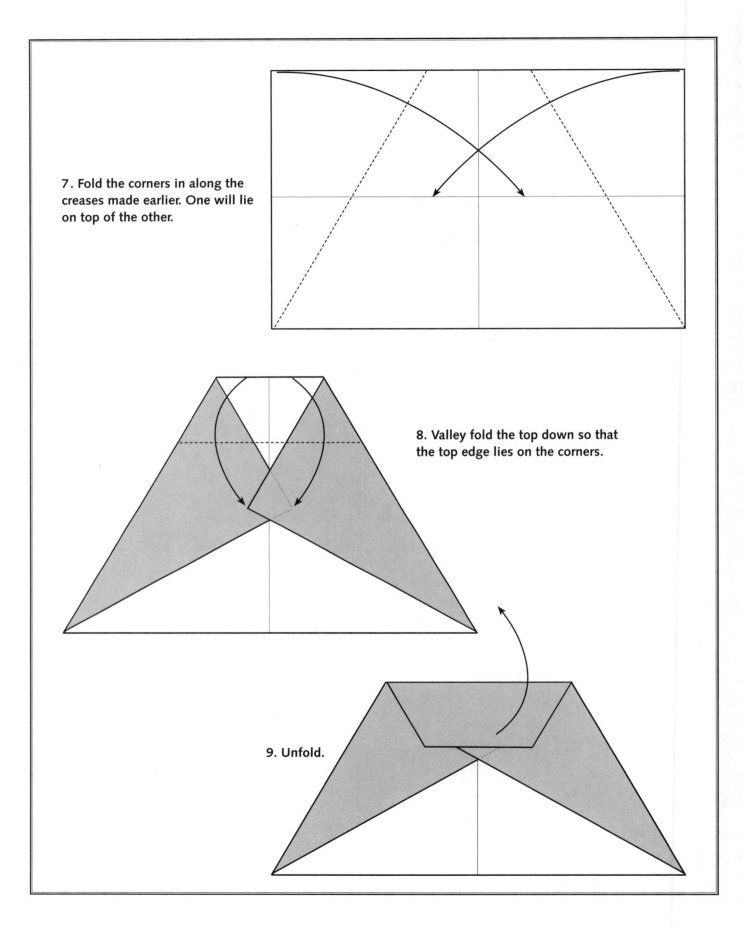

7. Fold the corners in along the creases made earlier. One will lie on top of the other.

8. Valley fold the top down so that the top edge lies on the corners.

9. Unfold.

24

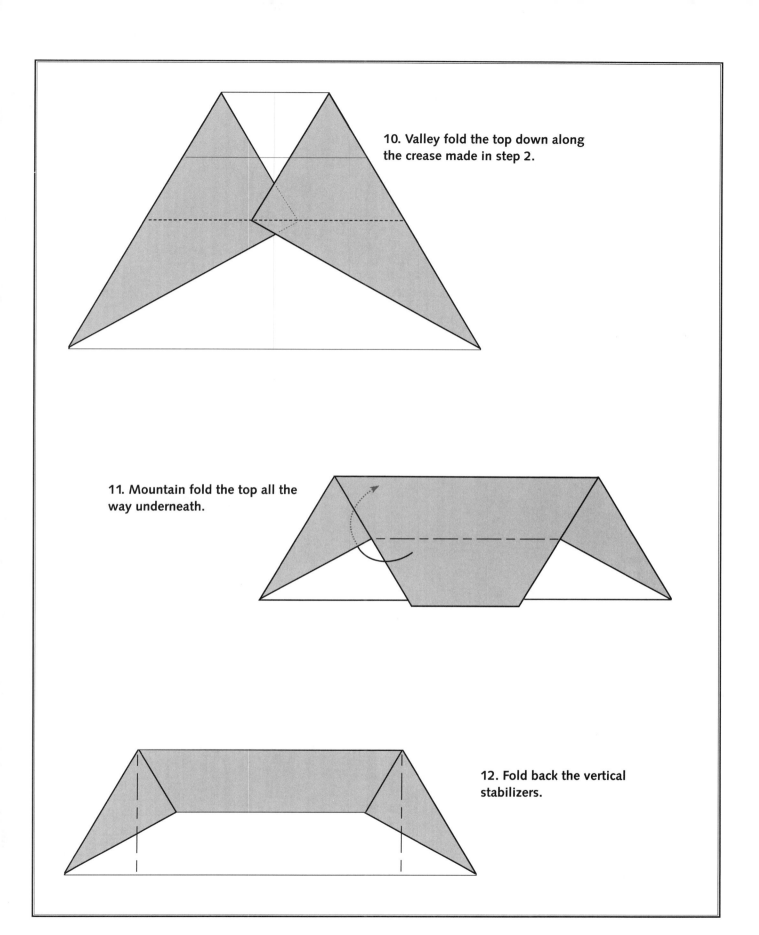

10. Valley fold the top down along the crease made in step 2.

11. Mountain fold the top all the way underneath.

12. Fold back the vertical stabilizers.

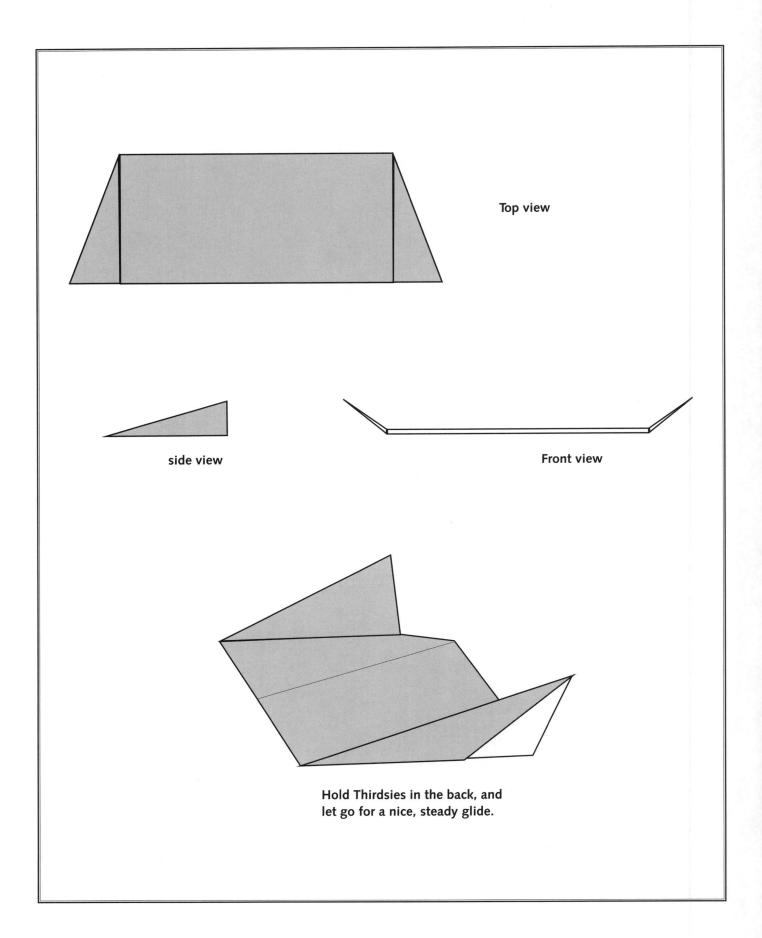

Top view

side view

Front view

Hold Thirdsies in the back, and
let go for a nice, steady glide.

26

Bottlenose

Start with an 8½ × 5½ inch
sheet of paper creased in half
lengthwise.

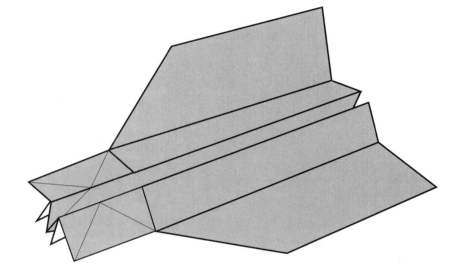

1.

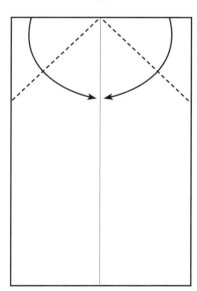

Valley fold so the top edges
meet the center line.

2.

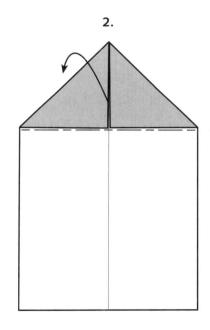

Mountain fold the top
section behind.

3.

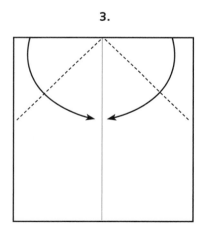

Valley fold so that the top
edges meet the center line.

4.

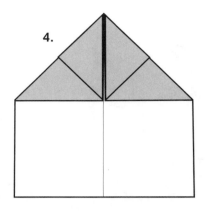

Turn over.

5.

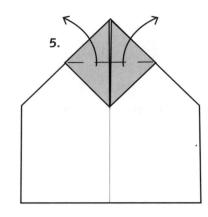

Open out the top section.

6.

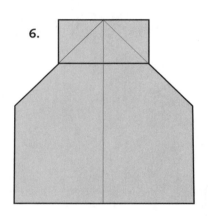

Turn over.

7.

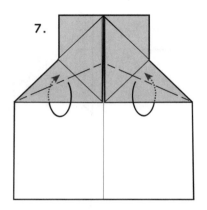

Mountain fold the flaps underneath to thicken the leading edges of the wing and move weight forward.

8.

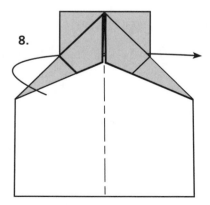

Mountain fold the model in half lengthwise.

9.

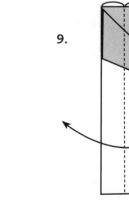

Valley fold the wings down by folding halfway across the top.

28

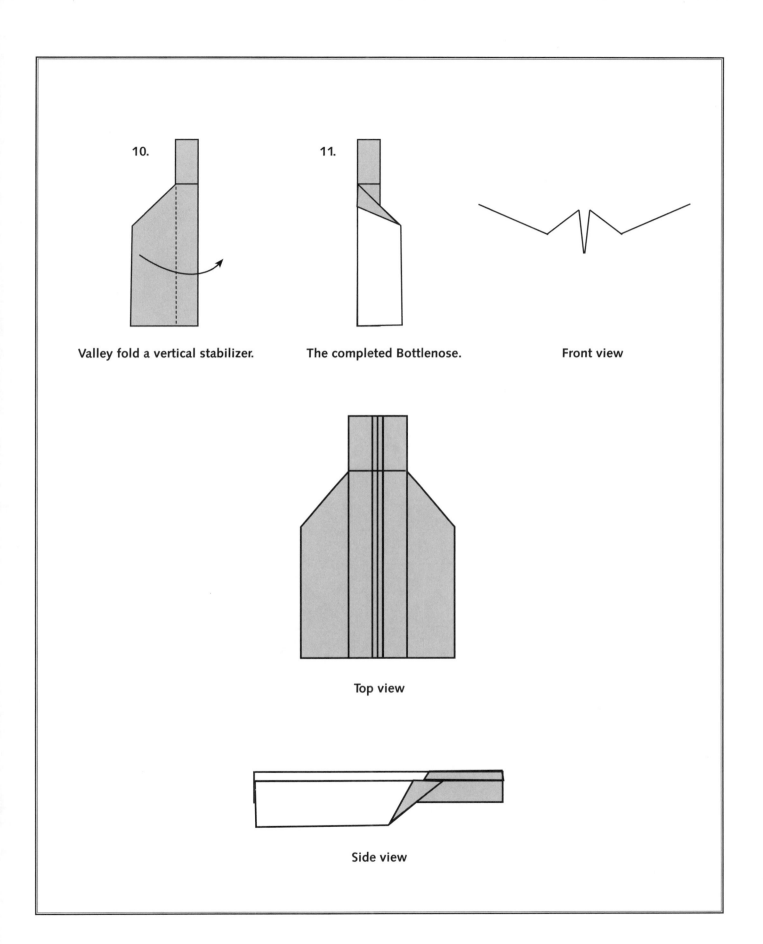

10.

Valley fold a vertical stabilizer.

11.

The completed Bottlenose.

Front view

Top view

Side view

Raptor

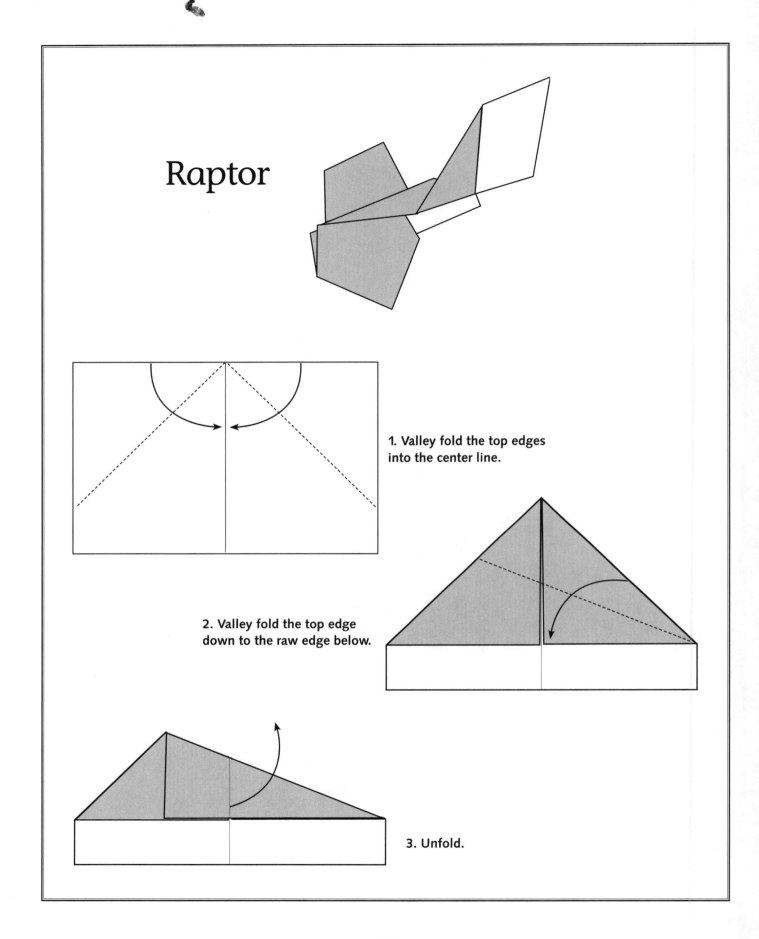

1. Valley fold the top edges into the center line.

2. Valley fold the top edge down to the raw edge below.

3. Unfold.

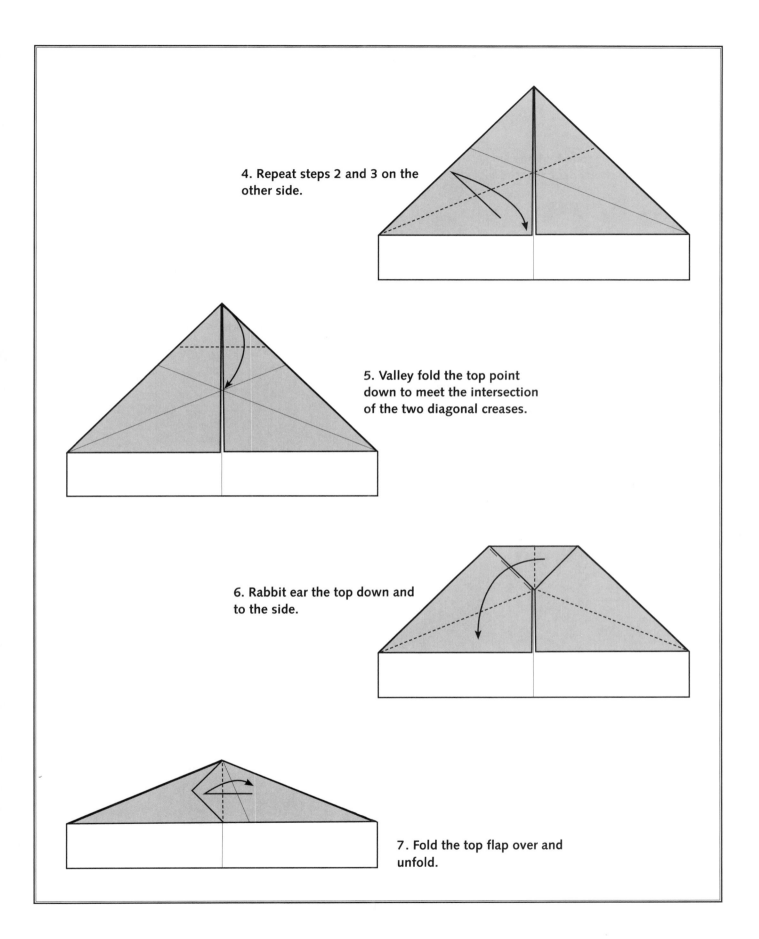

4. Repeat steps 2 and 3 on the other side.

5. Valley fold the top point down to meet the intersection of the two diagonal creases.

6. Rabbit ear the top down and to the side.

7. Fold the top flap over and unfold.

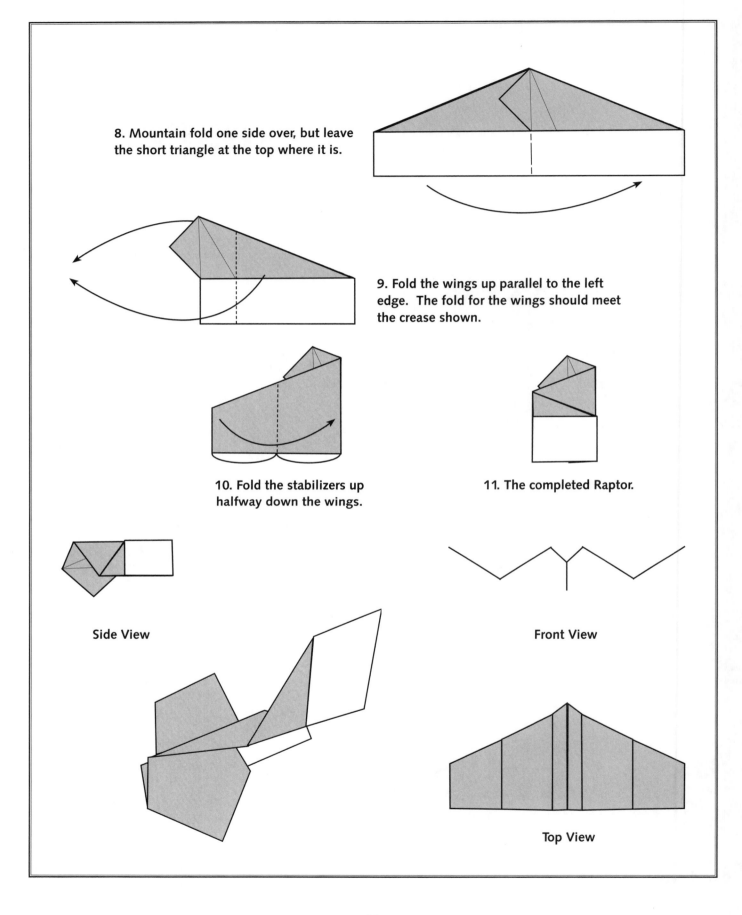

8. Mountain fold one side over, but leave the short triangle at the top where it is.

9. Fold the wings up parallel to the left edge. The fold for the wings should meet the crease shown.

10. Fold the stabilizers up halfway down the wings.

11. The completed Raptor.

Side View

Front View

Top View

Skeeter

Thrown hard or soft, Skeeter will give a good flight every time. The folding gets a little bit more complicated, though.

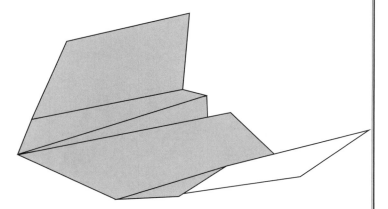

1.

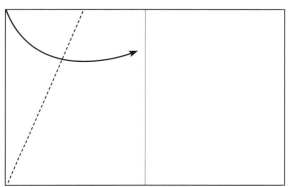

Valley fold so that the top corner lies on the center line. The fold should pass right through the bottom corner.

2. Like so. Repeat on the other side.

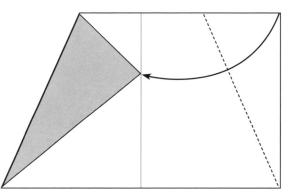

3.

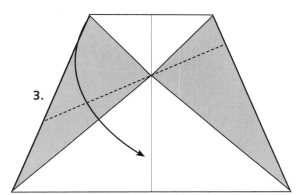

This gets a bit tricky. Valley fold so that the top left corner lies on the center line. Make sure that the fold runs through the intersection of the two flaps you just folded in.

4.

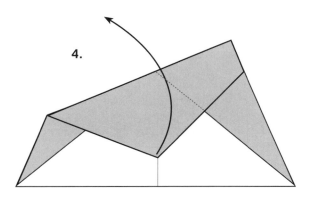

Unfold and repeat on the other side.

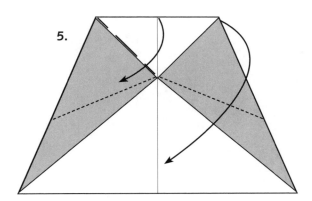

5.

Rabbit ear the top down and to the side using the creases made in the last two steps.

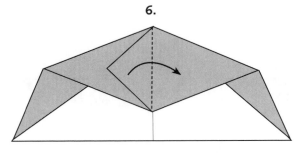

6.

Fold the top flap across and crease well.

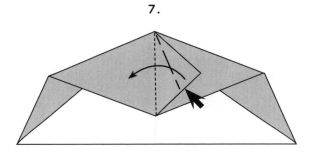

7.

Squash fold the flap to the other side.

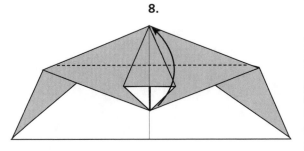

8.

Valley fold the bottom point of the top layer (it consists of paired white flaps) to the topmost point. Carefully fold through all the layers.

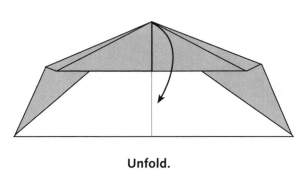

9.

Unfold.

10.

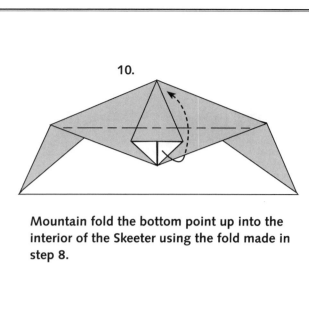

Mountain fold the bottom point up into the interior of the Skeeter using the fold made in step 8.

11.

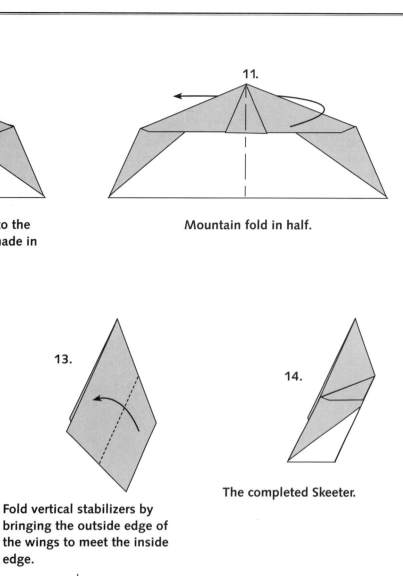

Mountain fold in half.

12.

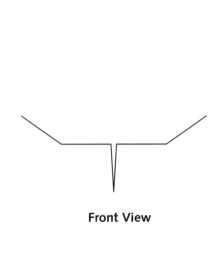

Fold the wings down following a line by the top layer in the front.

13.

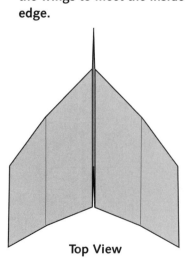

Fold vertical stabilizers by bringing the outside edge of the wings to meet the inside edge.

14.

The completed Skeeter.

Front View

Top View

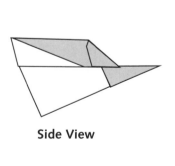

Side View

Glider Supreme

Start with an 8½ × 5½ inch sheet of paper creased in half lengthwise. The paper should always be creased in the middle to preserve symmetry.

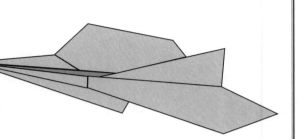

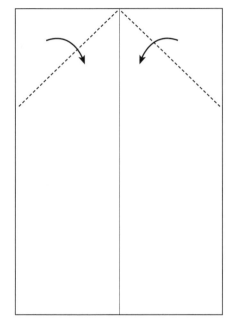

1.

Valley fold the corners so the top edge lies on the center line.

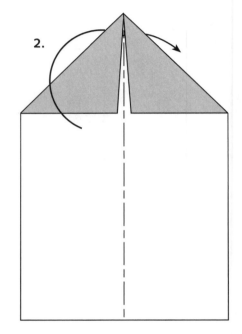

2.

Mountain fold in half.

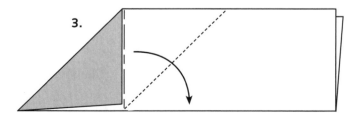

3.

Fold the triangular portion along the raw edge. The mountain fold should line up with the folded edge at the bottom.

4.

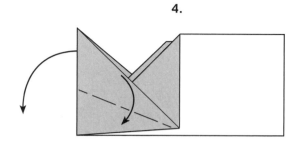

Outside reverse fold the triangle
in front.

5.

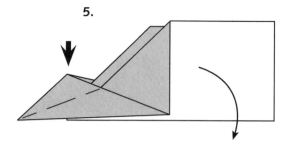

Open the model and flatten out
the forward portion.

6.

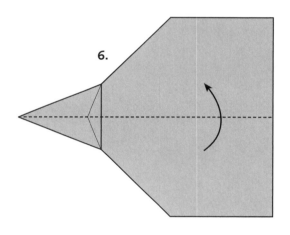

Valley fold in half.

7.

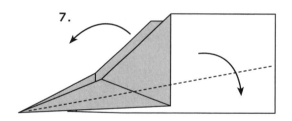

Bisecting the angle in front,
Valley fold the wings.

8.

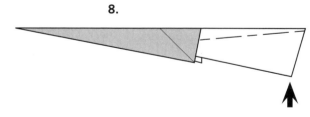

Inside reverse fold the tail as far
as it will go without resistance.

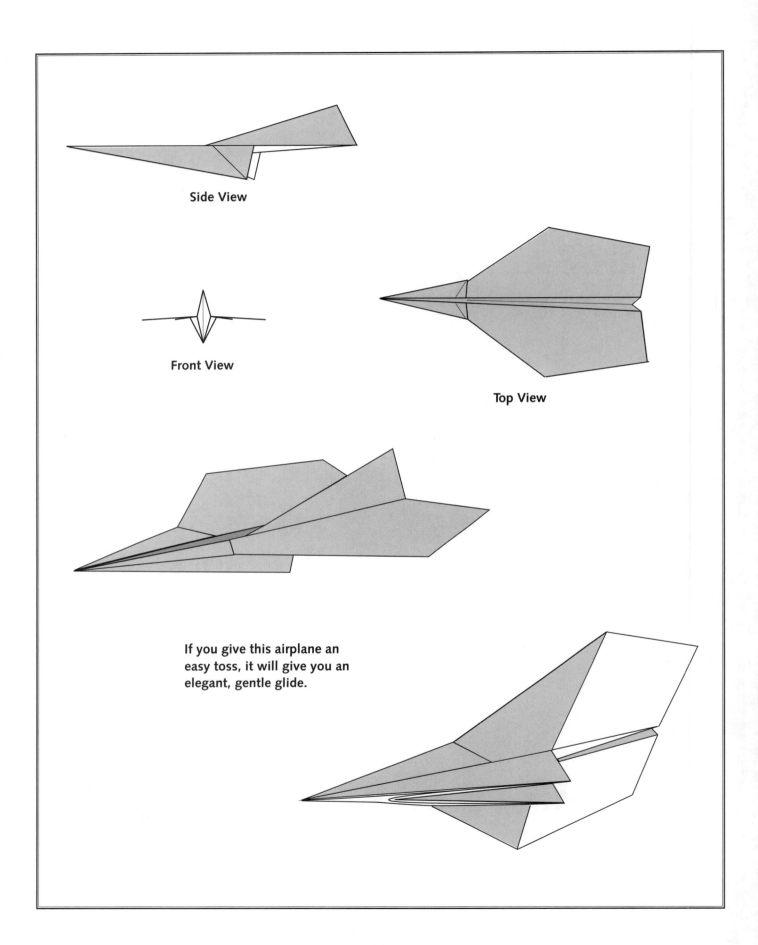

Side View

Front View

Top View

If you give this airplane an
easy toss, it will give you an
elegant, gentle glide.

Elapse

Elapse presents large control surfaces, and can be trimmed to do a great many things. Start with a sheet of paper creased in half lengthwise.

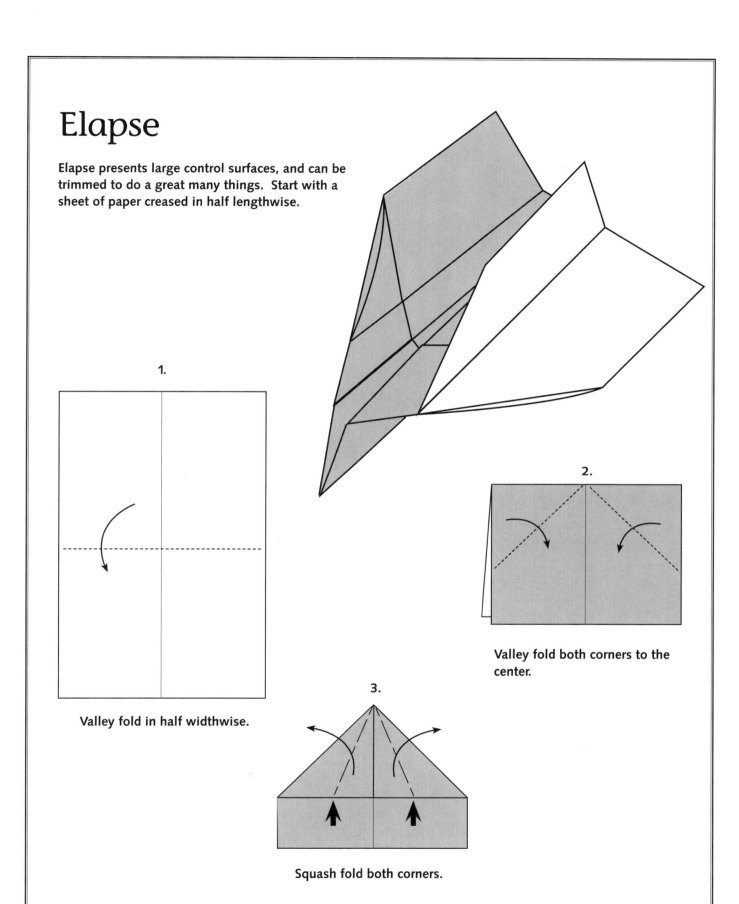

1.

Valley fold in half widthwise.

2.

Valley fold both corners to the center.

3.

Squash fold both corners.

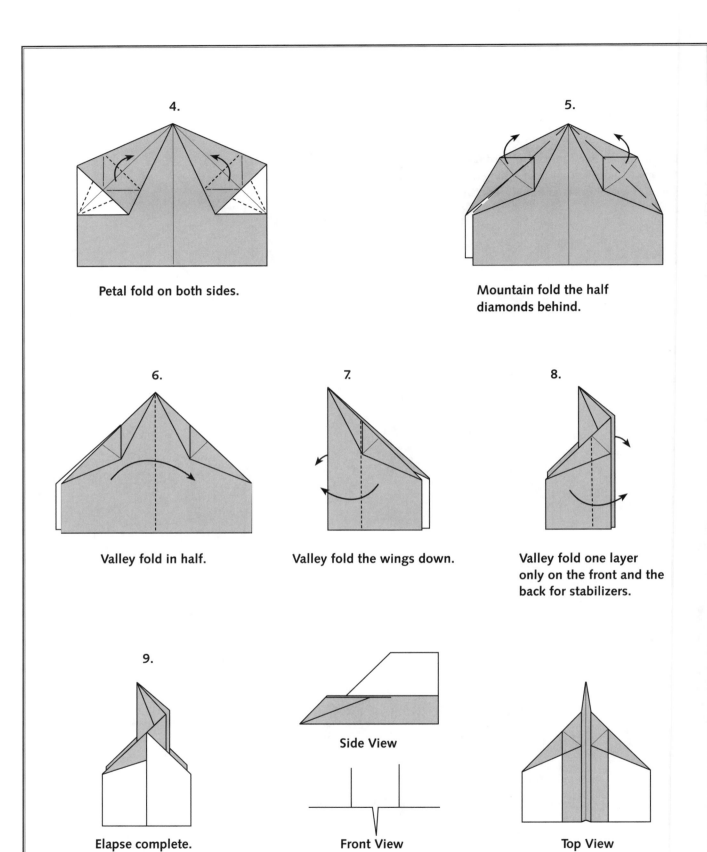

4.

Petal fold on both sides.

5.

Mountain fold the half
diamonds behind.

6.

Valley fold in half.

7.

Valley fold the wings down.

8.

Valley fold one layer
only on the front and the
back for stabilizers.

9.

Elapse complete.

Side View

Front View

Top View

F-14

This sleek design reminds me of an F-14 Tomcat in supersonic flight. Start with a sheet of paper folded in half and creased down the middle.

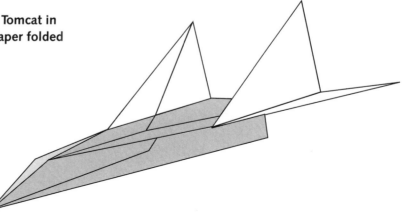

1.

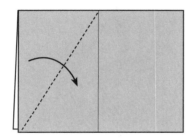

Valley fold from top center to bottom corner.

2.

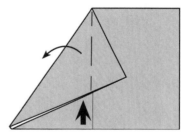

Squash fold the resulting flap.

3.

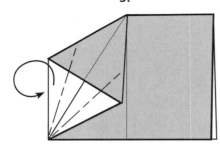

Mountain fold the flaps in half.

4.

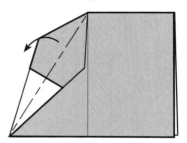

Mountain fold the half diamond behind.

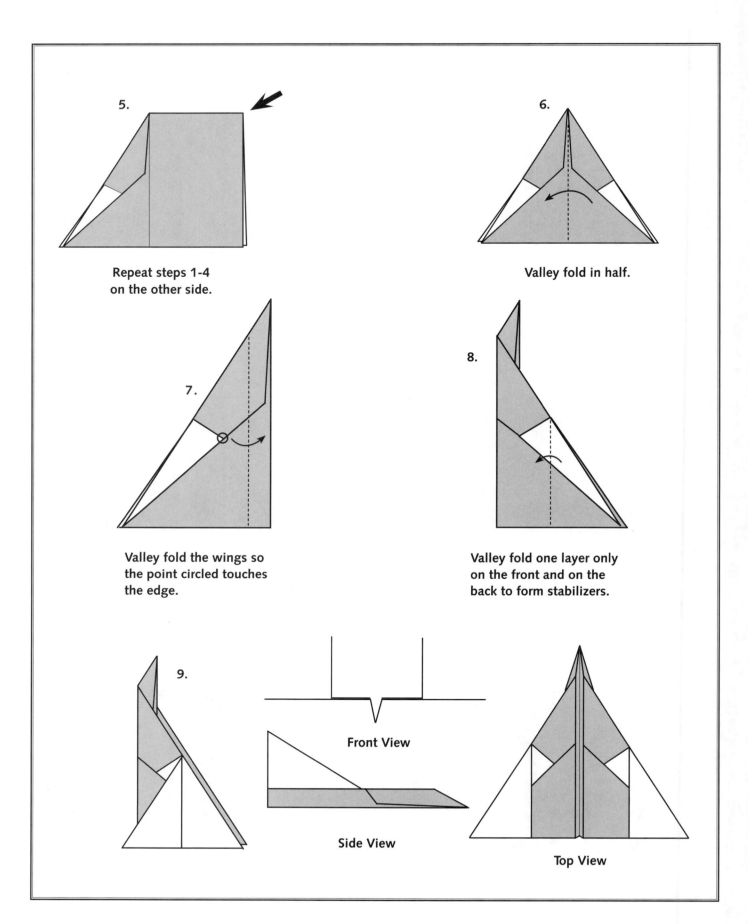

5.

Repeat steps 1-4
on the other side.

6.

Valley fold in half.

7.

Valley fold the wings so
the point circled touches
the edge.

8.

Valley fold one layer only
on the front and on the
back to form stabilizers.

9.

Front View

Side View

Top View

42

Omega Flyer

Another good stunt airplane; begin with the Airplane Base.

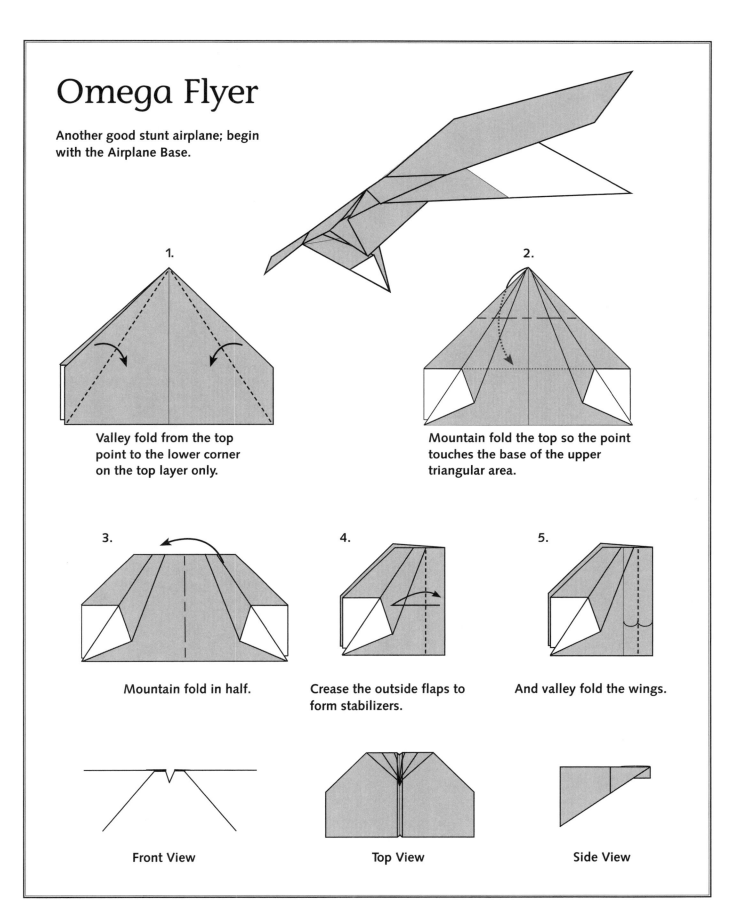

1.

Valley fold from the top point to the lower corner on the top layer only.

2.

Mountain fold the top so the point touches the base of the upper triangular area.

3.

Mountain fold in half.

4.

Crease the outside flaps to form stabilizers.

5.

And valley fold the wings.

Front View

Top View

Side View

Thin-layer
Aerodynamics

A collection of excellent paper airplanes. Be warned that the folding gets even more difficult from here!

Loopmaker

An excellent plane that can be adjusted to do all manner of stunts, including loops. Begin with the Canard Base.

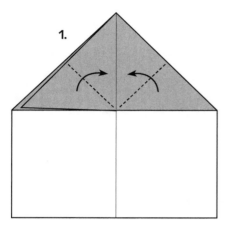

1.

This is in actuality a waterbomb base grafted on top of a rectangle and will be used for the next several airplanes. Valley fold the upper flaps in half.

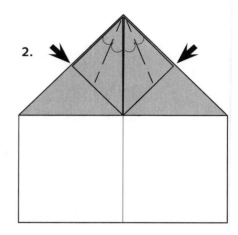

2.

Reverse fold in half.

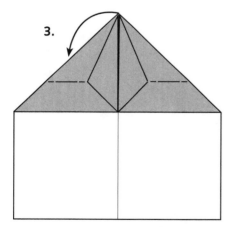

3.

Mountain fold the bottom point downward and behind as far as it will go.

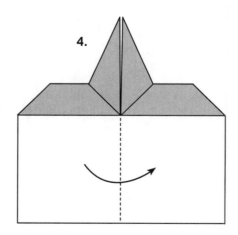

4.

Valley fold in half.

5.

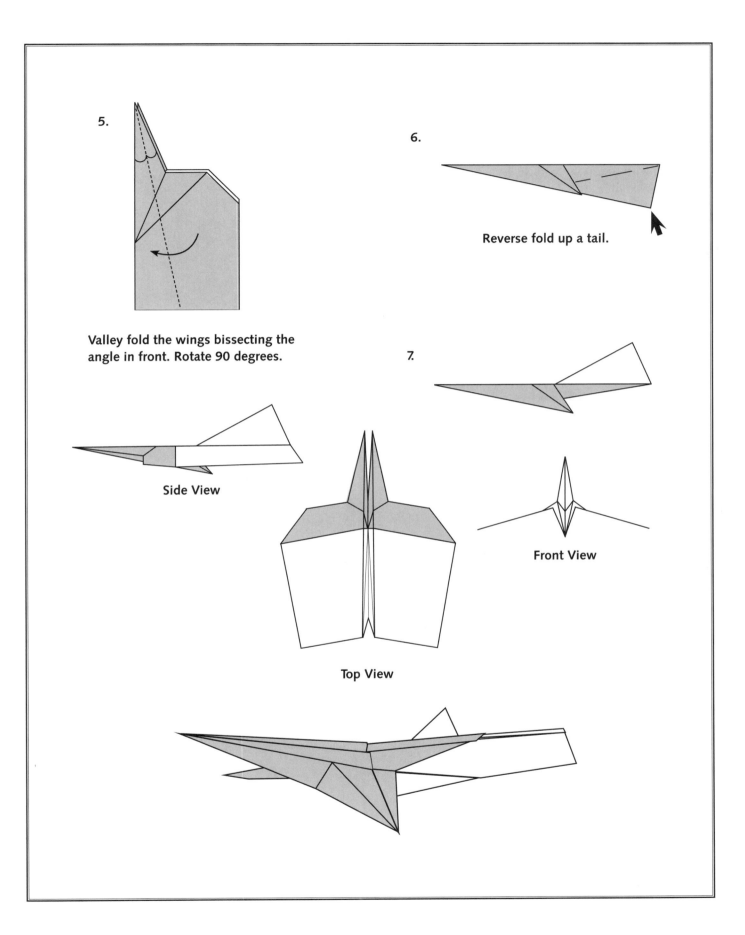

Valley fold the wings bissecting the angle in front. Rotate 90 degrees.

Side View

6.

Reverse fold up a tail.

7.

Front View

Top View

Mach II

This is one of my best flyers.
Start with the Airplane Base.

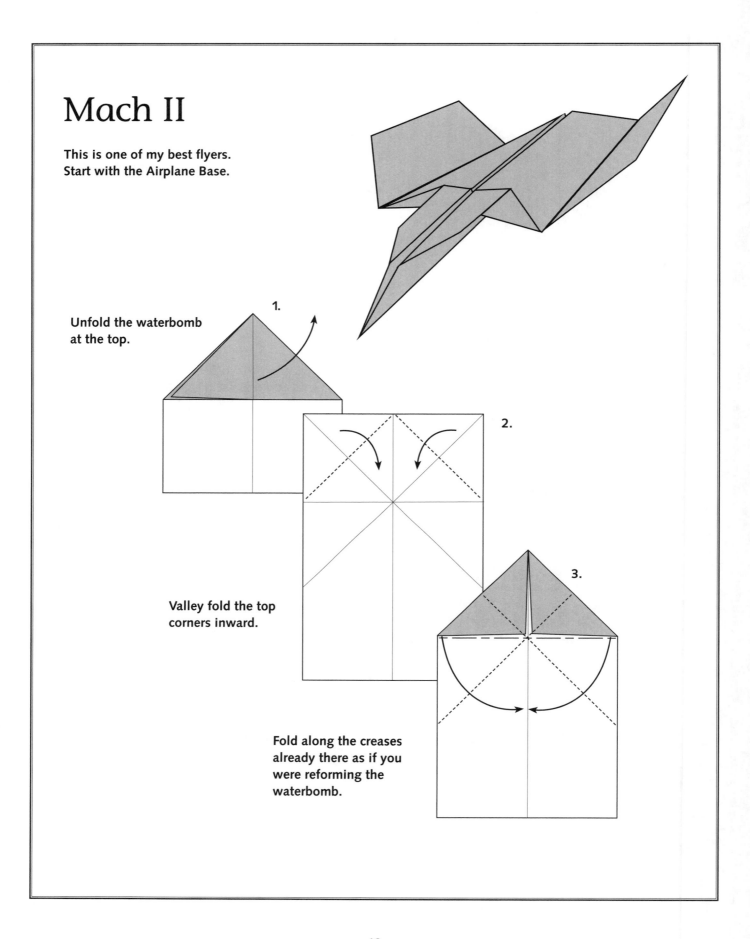

Unfold the waterbomb
at the top.

1.

2.

Valley fold the top
corners inward.

3.

Fold along the creases
already there as if you
were reforming the
waterbomb.

4.

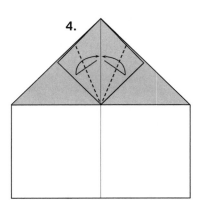

Fold the triangular flaps so their lower edges lie along the center line. Crease well, then unfold.

5.

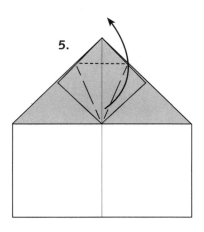

Petal fold the top layer upward.

6.

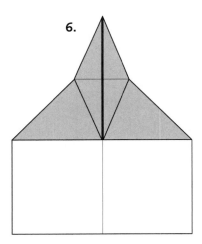

Turn the model over.

7.

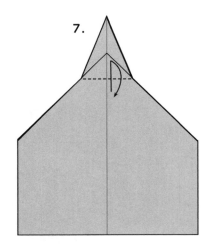

Valley fold the shorter of the two triangles at the top at its base. Crease well and unfold.

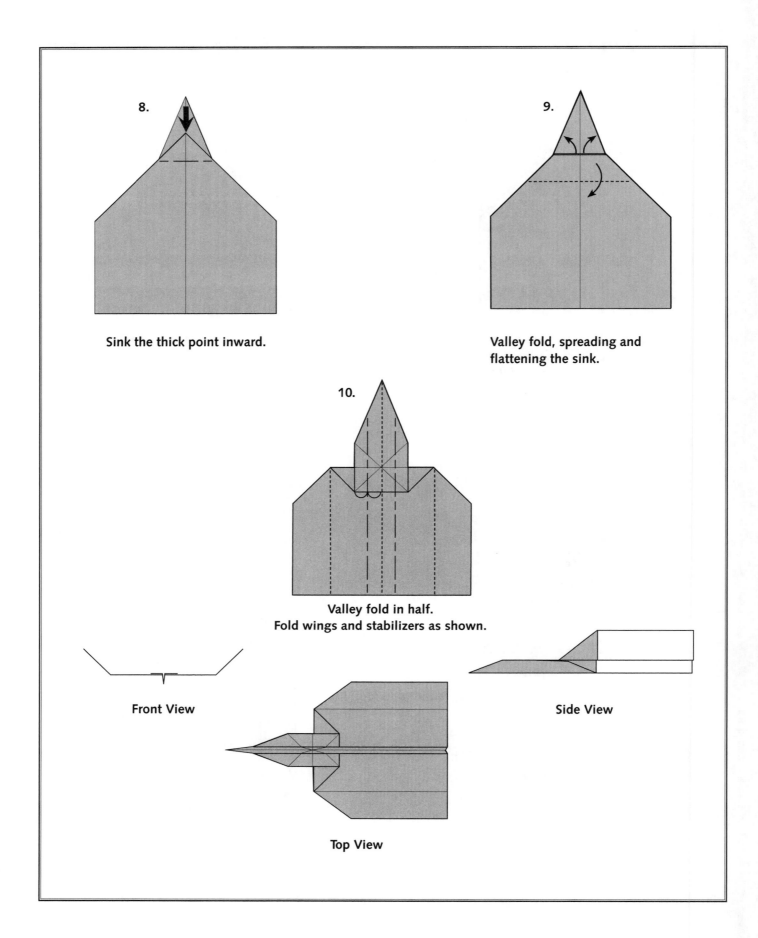

8. Sink the thick point inward.

9. Valley fold, spreading and flattening the sink.

10. Valley fold in half.
Fold wings and stabilizers as shown.

Front View

Top View

Side View

Multi-Stage Craft

Start with an 8½× 5½ inch sheet of paper creased down the middle.

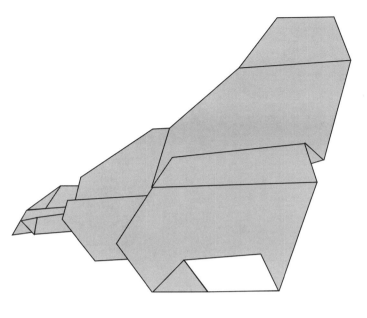

1.

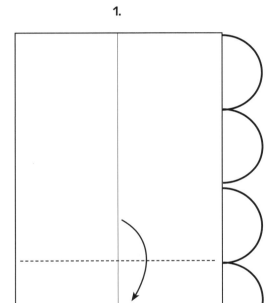

Valley fold ¾ of the paper down.

2.

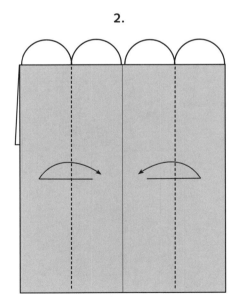

Valley fold into quarters. Unfold.

3.

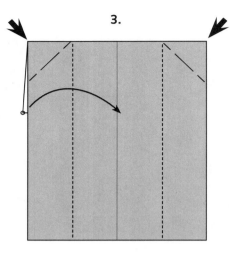

Valley fold the upper (long) layer while holding the bottom (short) layer in place, then squash fold the resulting upheaval.

4.

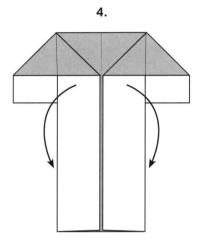

Fold the top layers underneath.

5.

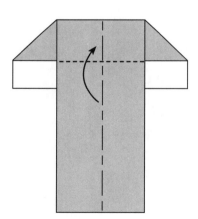

Valley fold the rectangular flap up as far as it will go. Mountain fold in half.

6.

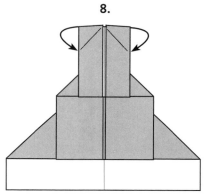

Valley fold the rectangle in half.

7.

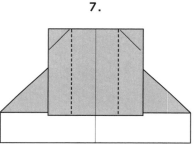

Repeat steps 3-5
on this section.

8.

Mountain fold the
top corners behind.

9.

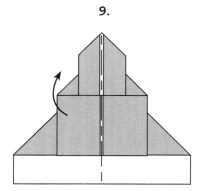

Mountain fold in half.

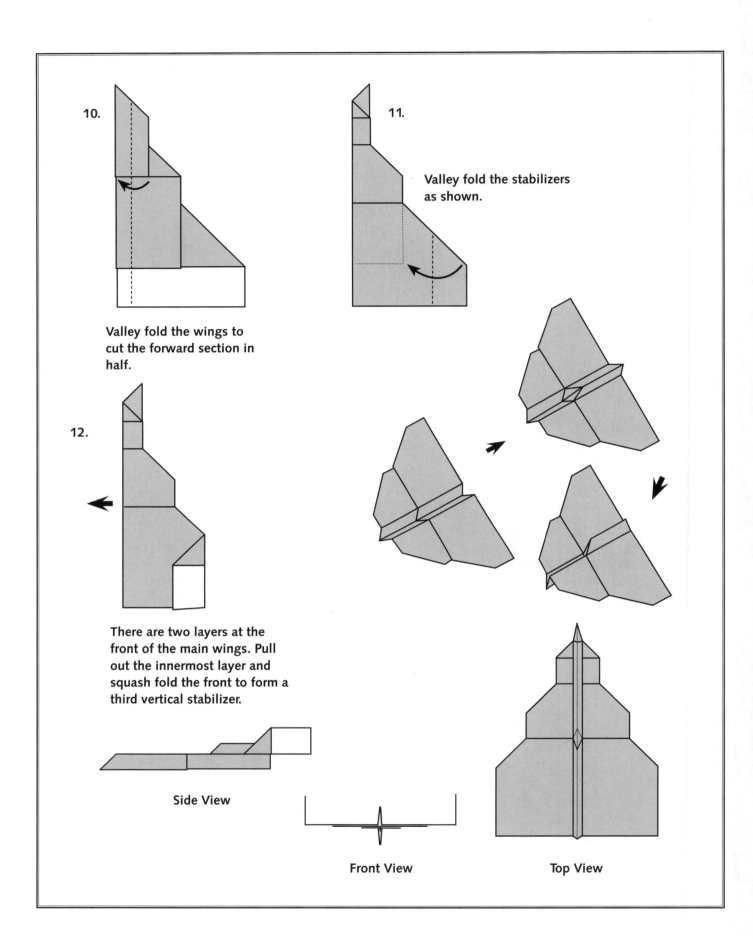

10.

Valley fold the wings to cut the forward section in half.

11.

Valley fold the stabilizers as shown.

12.

There are two layers at the front of the main wings. Pull out the innermost layer and squash fold the front to form a third vertical stabilizer.

Side View

Front View

Top View

Thunderbird

The idea here is the same as the previous design, but the effect is quite different. Start with an 8½ × 5½ inch sheet of paper from which you will make a trapezoid.

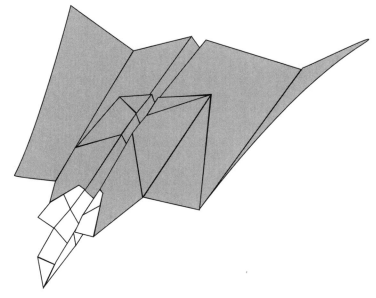

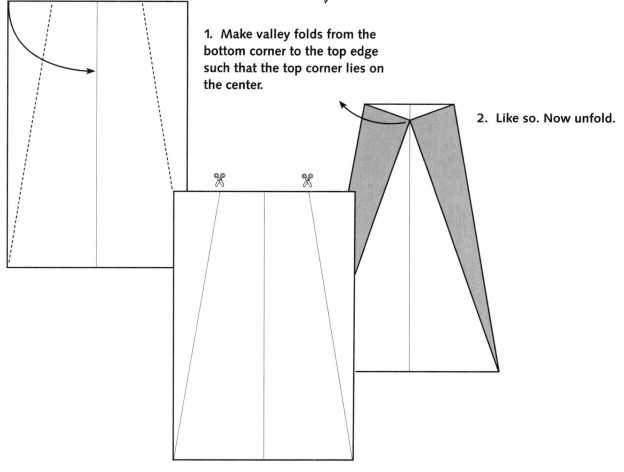

1. Make valley folds from the bottom corner to the top edge such that the top corner lies on the center.

2. Like so. Now unfold.

3. Cut, tear, or otherwise rend along these creases to remove the triangular flaps.

4.

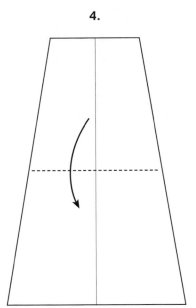

Valley fold in half.

5.

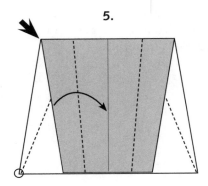

This is similar to step 3 of the Multi-Stage Craft. Hold the bottom layer down while valley folding the top layer so the raw edge lies flush with the center. A pocket will form; squash this. Continue the squash with a valley fold on the lower layer down to the bottom corner.

6.

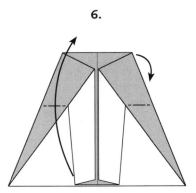

Mountain fold the top down and behind. The trapezoid at the bottom flips up.

7.

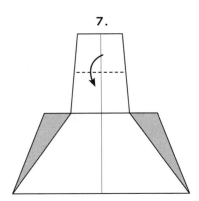

Valley fold the top part in half.

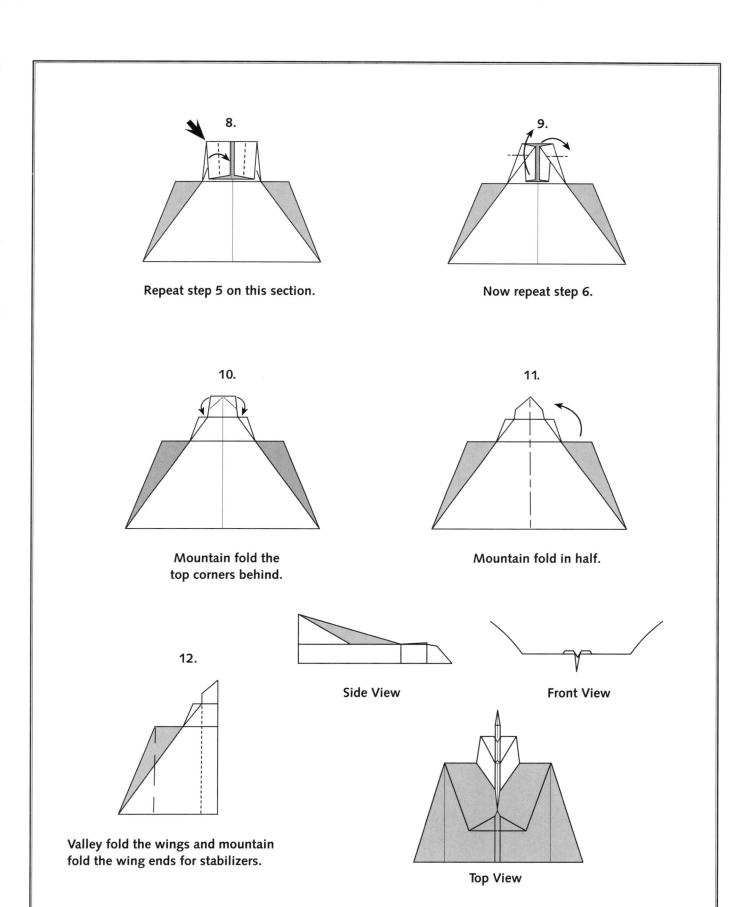

8.

Repeat step 5 on this section.

9.

Now repeat step 6.

10.

Mountain fold the
top corners behind.

11.

Mountain fold in half.

12.

Valley fold the wings and mountain
fold the wing ends for stabilizers.

Side View

Front View

Top View

Coriolis Max

This elegant glider is one of my favorites. A medium-hard or hard throw will give you a great flight. Begin with a sheet of paper creased down the middle.

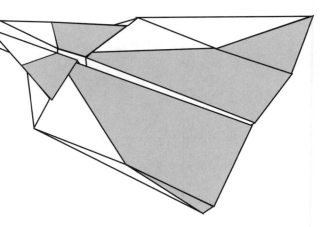

1.

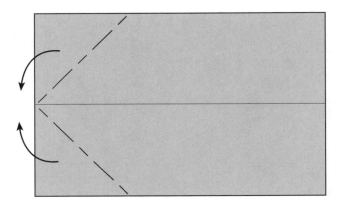

Mountain fold the corners to the center.

2.

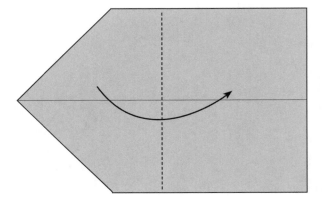

Valley fold in half.

3.

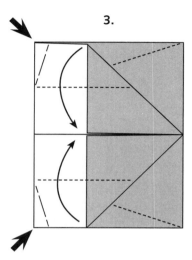

Squash fold the sides inward
as in step 5 of the Thunderbird.

4a.

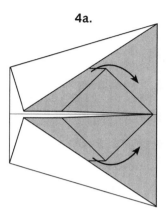

Fold the top layers underneath
as in step 4 of the Multi-Stage
Craft.

4b.

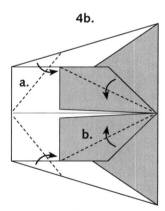

Valley folds:

a. From the top center to the
edge. The outside edge should
lie on the point shown.

b. Point to point.

5.

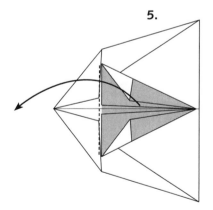

Valley fold the triangular flap
forward.

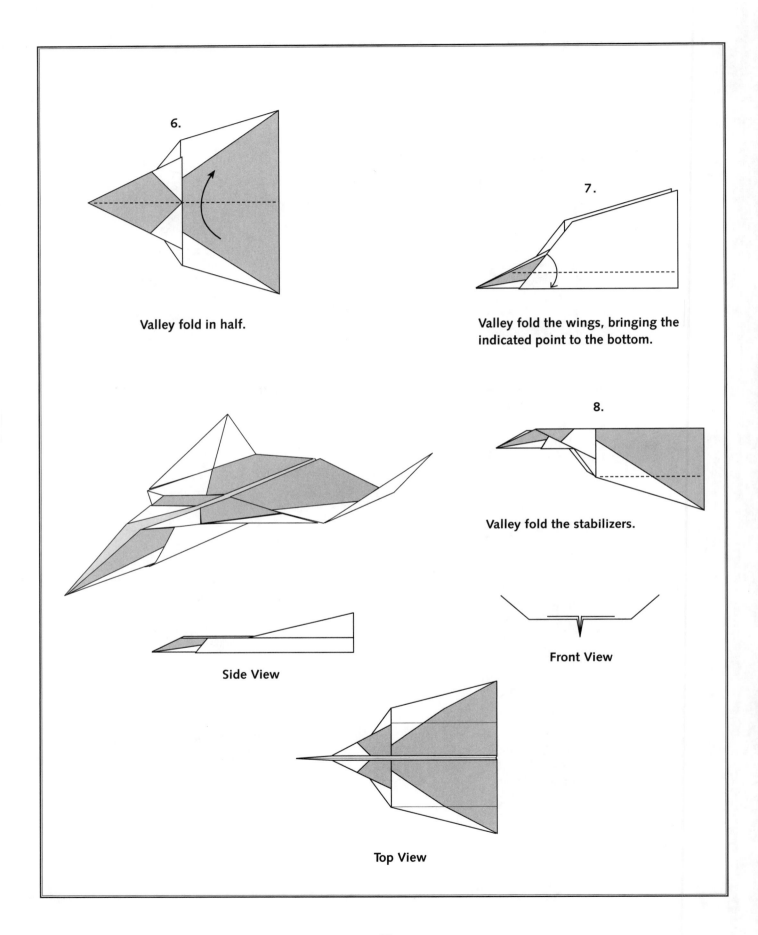

6.

Valley fold in half.

7.

Valley fold the wings, bringing the indicated point to the bottom.

8.

Valley fold the stabilizers.

Side View

Front View

Top View

Pocket Aerobat

Like any good stunt plane, this will fly as
well upside-down as right-side up. Begin
with the Airplane Base.

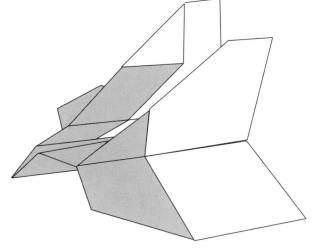

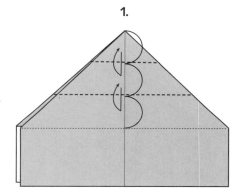

1.

Divide the upper triangle into thirds.

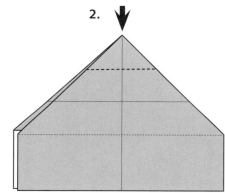

2.

Sink the upper third.

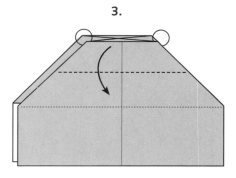

3.

Valley fold the top layer down along
the 2/3 crease while holding the
bottom layer still. Two flaps on the
inside will open up and form a square.

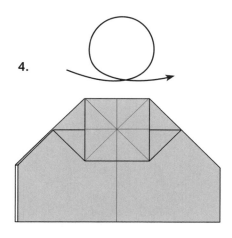

4.

Turn over.

5.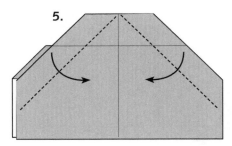

Valley fold the top layer so the folded edge on top lies flush with the center line.

6.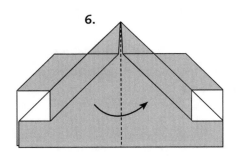

Valley fold in half.

7.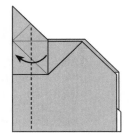

Valley fold the wings down.

8.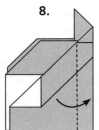

Fold up the stabilizers, one layer only.

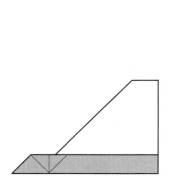

Side View

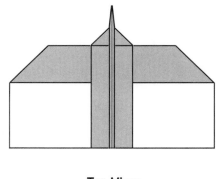

Top View

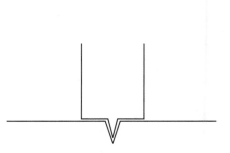

Front View

Canards

Real canards take advantage of a forward wing configuration, which assists in maneuvering and can help avoid stalls — situations when the airplane is pointed too high (a high "angle of attack") and the air flow decreases over the wing. Stalls are most common during takeoffs and landings, when the airplane is moving at slow speed and maneuvering constantly. In canards, the front wing will usually stall out before the main wings, automatically decreasing the angle of attack and preventing this very dangerous condition. This section contains many of the airplanes made from the canard base and a few that aren't.

Aerobotch

This ungainly little plane makes a superb dart. Its large control surfaces can also be used to create many maneuvers and stunts. Start with the Airplane Base.

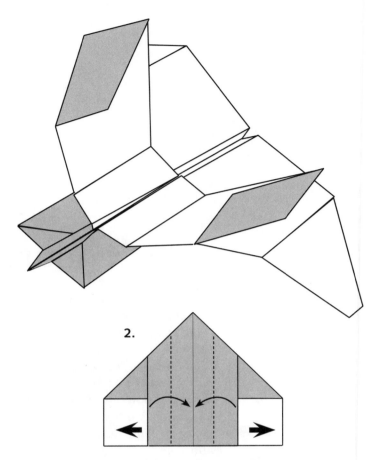

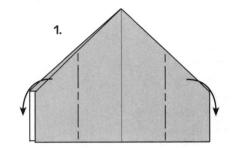

1.

Mountain fold the upper flaps in half.

2.

Valley fold in half again, allowing the flaps underneath to flip out.

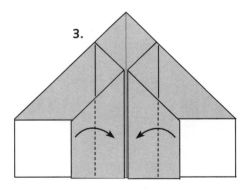

3.

Valley fold in half once again.

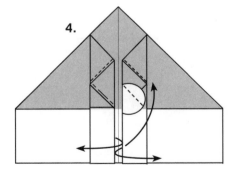

4.

Now for the fun part: Squash fold the top layer upward following the upper diagonal folds. At the same time you'll have to squash fold a pocket that forms underneath.

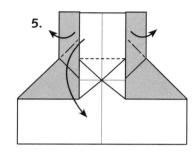

5.

Squash fold the upper flap
downward.

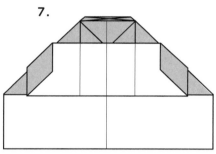

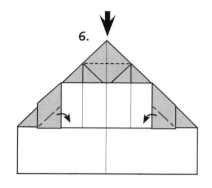

6.

Tuck the two corners underneath
the side flaps and sink the top.

7.

Turn the model over.

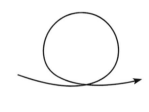

8.

Valley fold and open out as in Step
5 of the Pocket Aerobat.

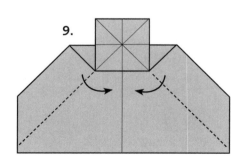

9.

Reverse fold so that the folded
edge on top lies on the center.

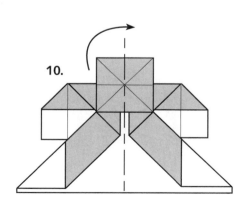

10.

Mountain fold in half.

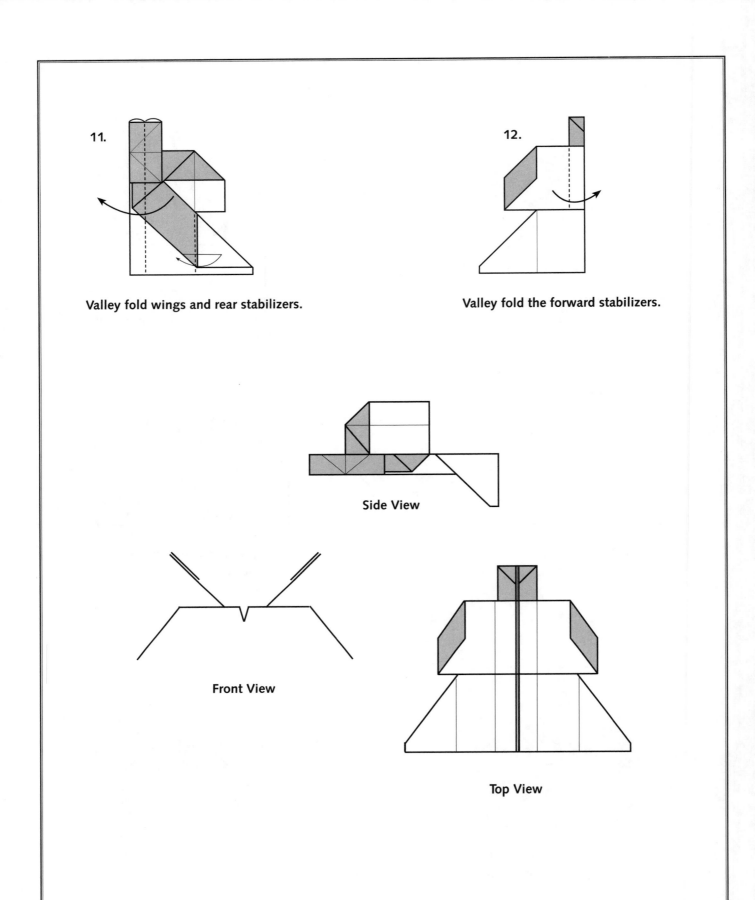

11.

Valley fold wings and rear stabilizers.

12.

Valley fold the forward stabilizers.

Side View

Front View

Top View

Pleator Volant

The folding method here is similar to the Pocket Aerobat. Begin with the Canard Base.

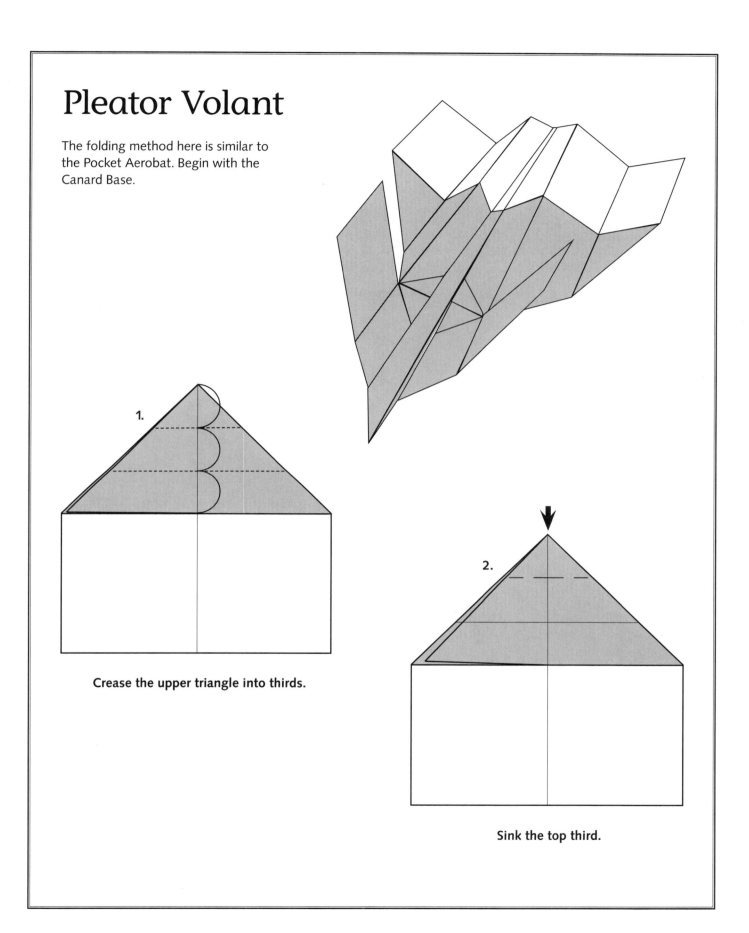

1.

Crease the upper triangle into thirds.

2.

Sink the top third.

3.

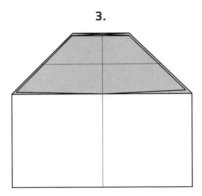

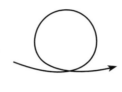

Turn the model over.

4.

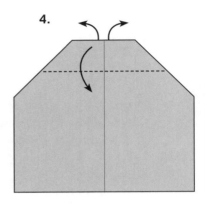

Valley fold and open out as in
Step 5 of the Pocket Aerobat.

5.

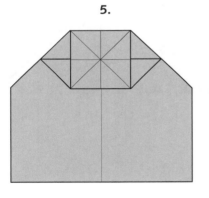

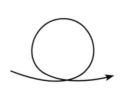

Turn the model over.

6.

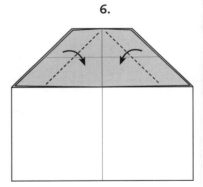

Valley fold so that the top edge
lies on the center line.

7.

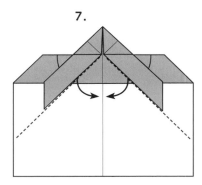

Repeat on the lower part of the model. The top edge will travel under the upper layer.

8.

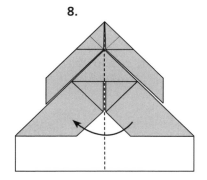

Valley fold in half.

9.

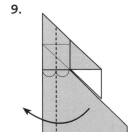

Valley fold the wings.

10.

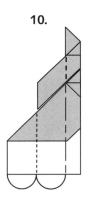

Valley fold the forward wings up. Mountain fold the wings down at their bases and up at their ends.

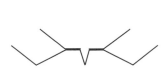

Front View

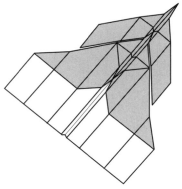

Top View

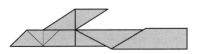

Side View

Hammerhead

For this canard begin with Step 2 of the Loopmaker.

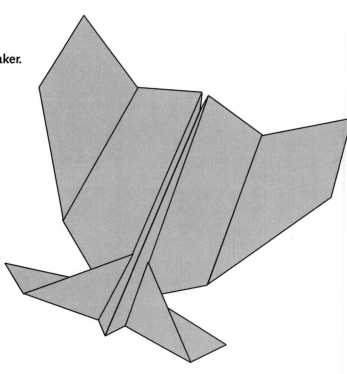

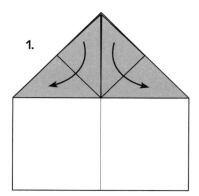

1.

Unfold the top flaps.

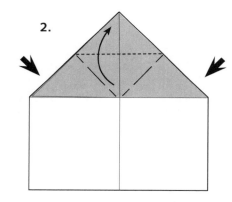

2.

Petal fold the upper layer.

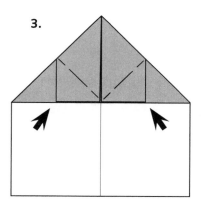

3.

Reverse fold the bottom corners inward.

4.

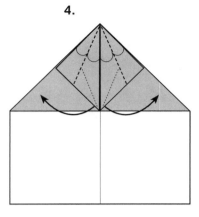

Bisecting the angles at the top, squash fold the upper flaps to the outside.

5.

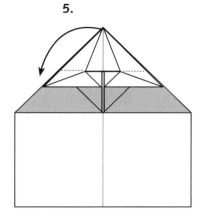

There are two points at the top. Mountain fold the lower flap (the one not visible in the drawing) down as far as it will go.

6.

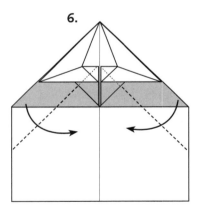

Valley fold to form the forward edges of the wings so that the top edge of the wing section (which lies between two layers and is not visible in the diagram) touches the center line.

7.

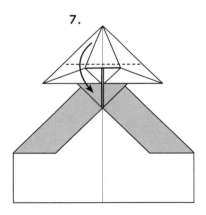

Valley fold the top point down.

8.

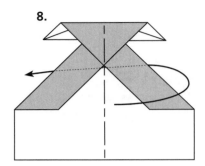

Mountain fold in half.

9.

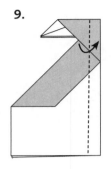

Valley fold the wings.

10.

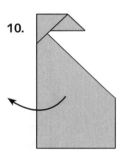

Unfold one side.

11.

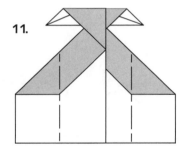

Mountain fold the stabilizers.

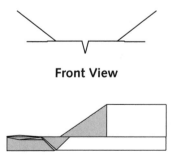

Front View

Side View

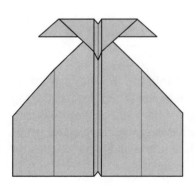

Top View

72

Pagodor Volant

A long time ago I tried mounting a traditional Chinese pagoda on the end of a rectangle to make an airplane. What I got was this interesting delta-winged canard with a trick front end. Begin (once again) with Loopmaker, Step 2.

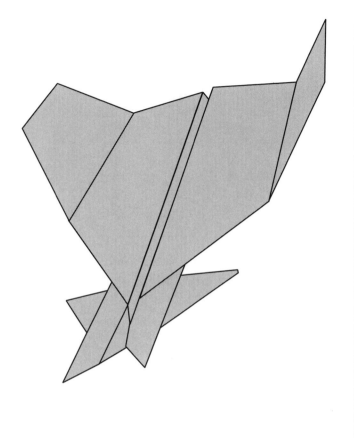

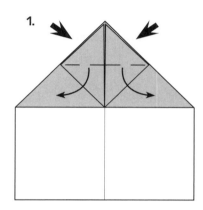

1.

Squash fold the uppermost flaps.

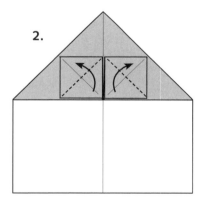

2.

Valley fold upward
the top layer only.

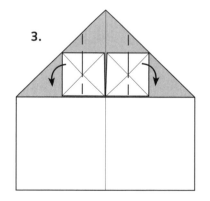

3.

Mountain fold the upper flaps in half.

4.

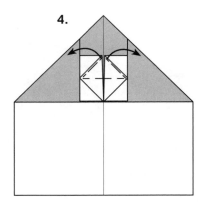

Spread the flaps on top apart. This will create a pocket that can be easily flattened.

5.

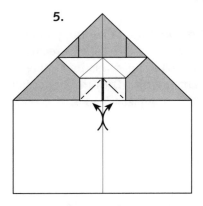

Reverse fold both corners inward.

6.

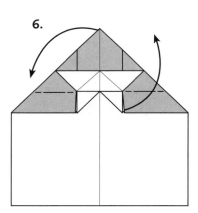

Flip so that the point at the top goes behind and the two small triangles flip upward.

7.

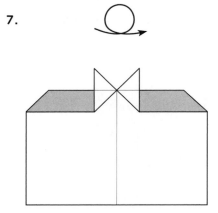

Turn the model over.

8.

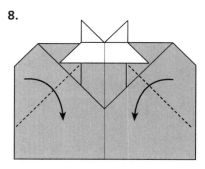

Valley fold so the folded edge on top lies on the center (this fold is similar to Step 5 of the Hammerhead).

9.

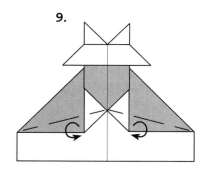

Mountain fold the trailing edges of the wing undersides behind.

10.

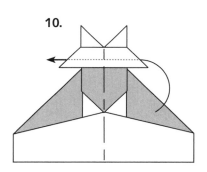

Mountain fold in half.

11.

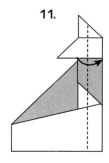

Valley fold the wings.

12.

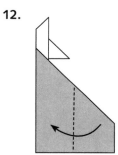

Valley fold the stabilizers.

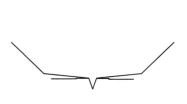

Front View

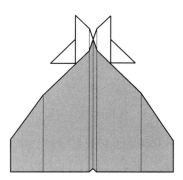

Top View

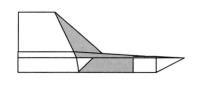

Side View

Jolly Roger

This amiable little airplane begins with the Canard Base. It also uses one of the nastiest sink folds in origami. Good luck.

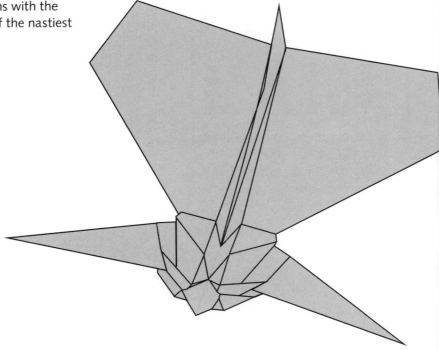

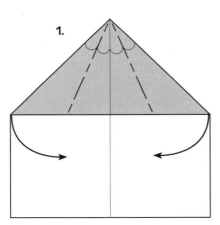

1.

Reverse fold the triangular flaps in half.

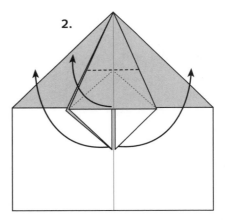

2.

Squash fold the two triangular flaps out to the side while valley folding the top layer upward.

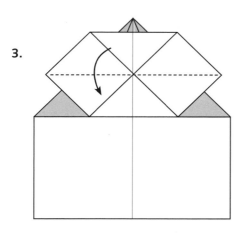

3.

Valley fold the top half of the
spread-out region back down.

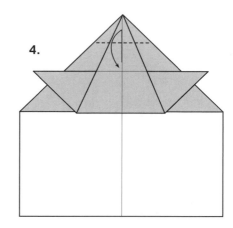

4.

Valley fold the top corner to the
front of the forward wings. Crease
well, and unfold.

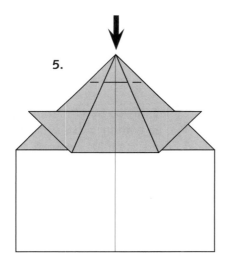

5.

This is the killer sink fold referred
to earlier.

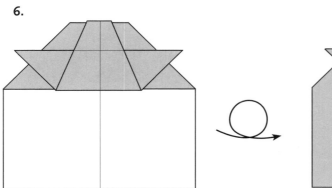

6.

Turn the model over.

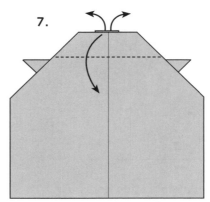

7.

Valley fold and spread
out the sink.

8.

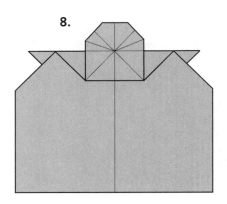

Turn over again.

9.

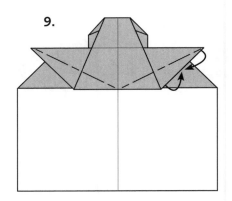

Narrow the forward wings with mountain folds in front and valley folds behind.

10.

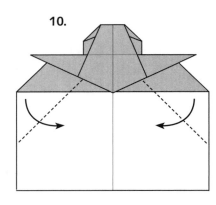

Valley fold so that the top edges line up with the center. Be careful to make the folds symmetrically, as they will form the leading edges of the wings.

11.

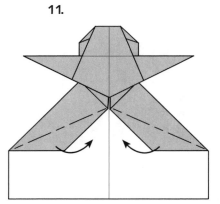

Using mountain folds from base to tip, narrow the leading edges of the wings.

12.

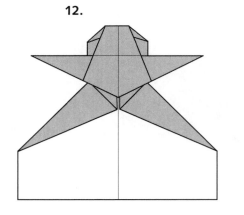

Turn the model over.

13.

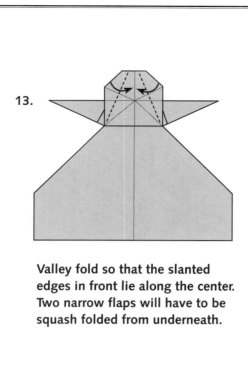

Valley fold so that the slanted edges in front lie along the center. Two narrow flaps will have to be squash folded from underneath.

14.

Valley fold the nose and insert it into the pockets below.

15.

Valley fold in half.

16.

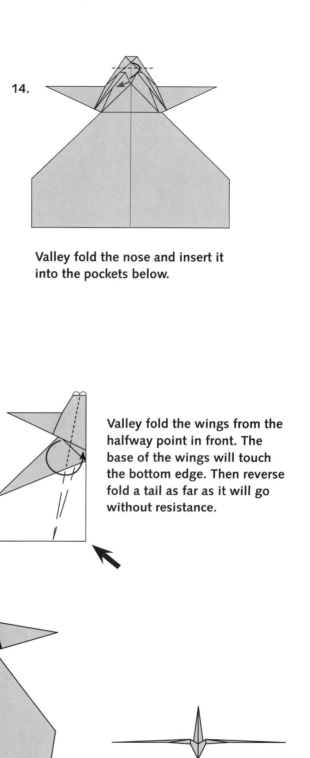

Valley fold the wings from the halfway point in front. The base of the wings will touch the bottom edge. Then reverse fold a tail as far as it will go without resistance.

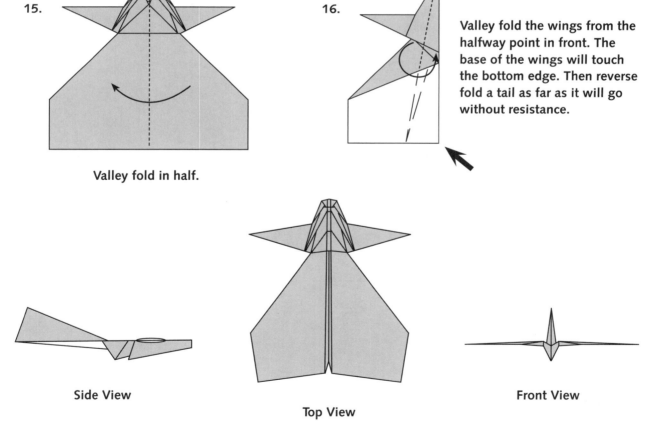

Side View

Top View

Front View

Bombwielder

OK, so it's not a canard, but it bombs stuff. Capable of delivering a payload of semi-guided missiles or bombs, this design contains some of the toughest origami around. Start with the Canard Base.

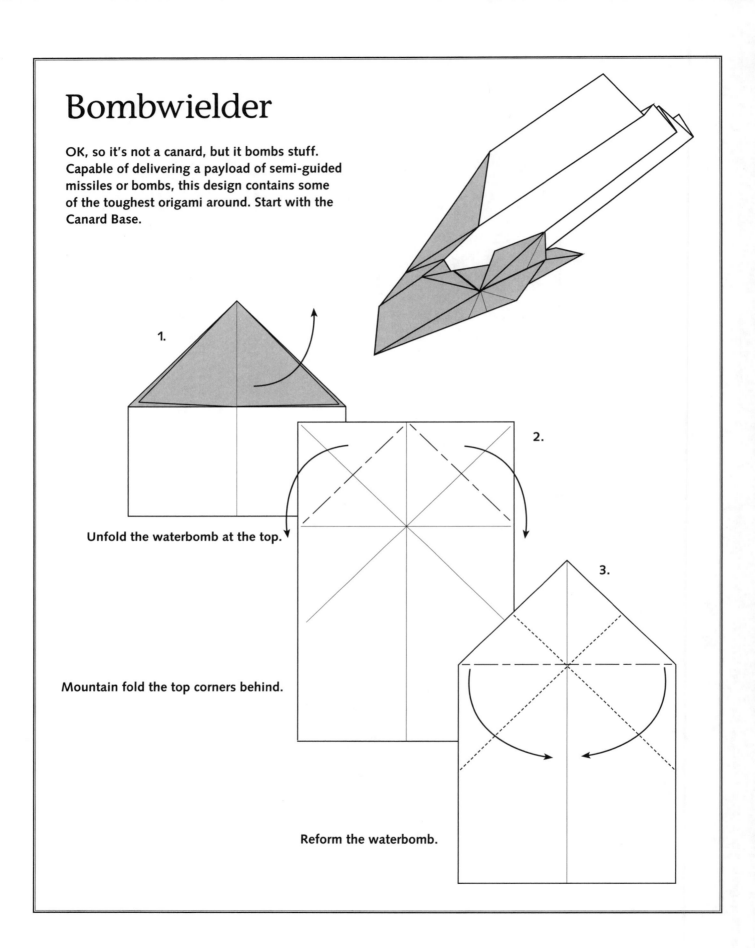

1.

Unfold the waterbomb at the top.

2.

Mountain fold the top corners behind.

3.

Reform the waterbomb.

4.

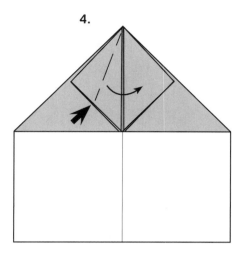

Squash fold the left flap to the right.

5.

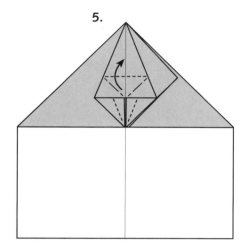

Petal fold.

6.

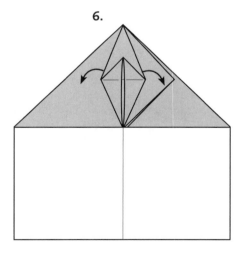

The diamond created in the last two steps is composed of two layers. Pull the outside layer loose from around the diamond and flatten it out.

7.

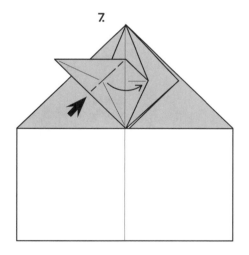

Squash fold the large triangle.

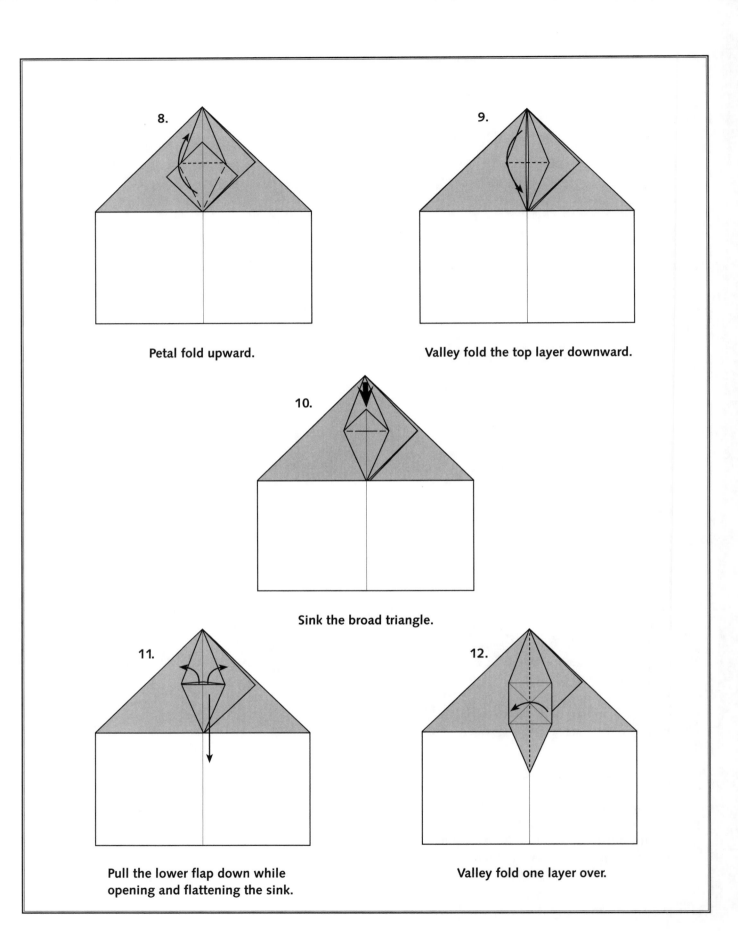

13.

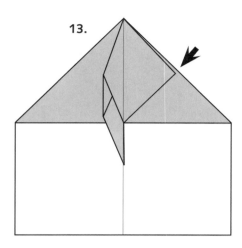

Repeat Steps 4–11 on the other side.

14.

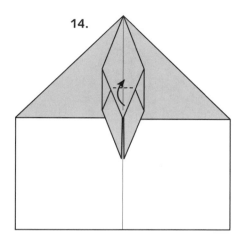

Valley fold the small triangle upward.

15.

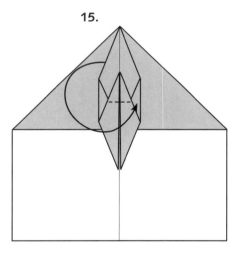

Valley fold two layers to the right.

16.

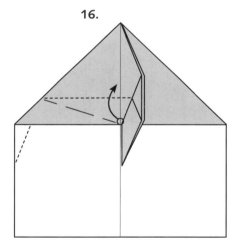

Squash fold upward. Keep the point marked with a circle on the center line.

17.

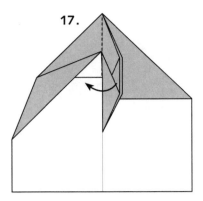

Valley fold one layer over.

18.

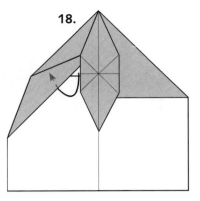

There are now three layers. Reverse fold the middle layer to the inside; this should lock the other two layers together.

19.

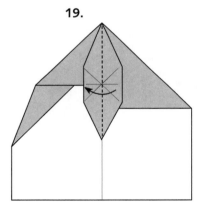

Valley fold one layer over.

20.

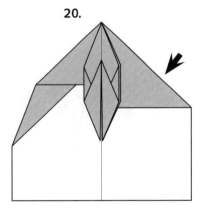

Repeat steps 15–19 on the other sides. Be sure to keep the two sides even; it's easy to lose symmetry at this point.

21.

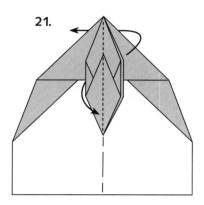

Valley fold one layer of the war pod to the right, and mountain fold one wing to the left.

22.

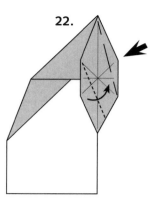

Valley fold the rear of the war pod over as far as it will go. Sink the front of the war pod from corner to corner on one side only.

23.

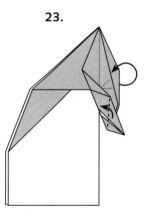

Valley fold the lower front of the war pod and tuck it into the pocket formed in the previous step. Valley fold the lower rear flap so that it stands straight up (perpendicular to the rest).

24.

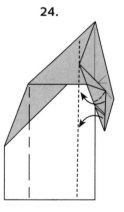

Open out the bomb bays. Valley fold the wings, and mountain fold the stabilizers.

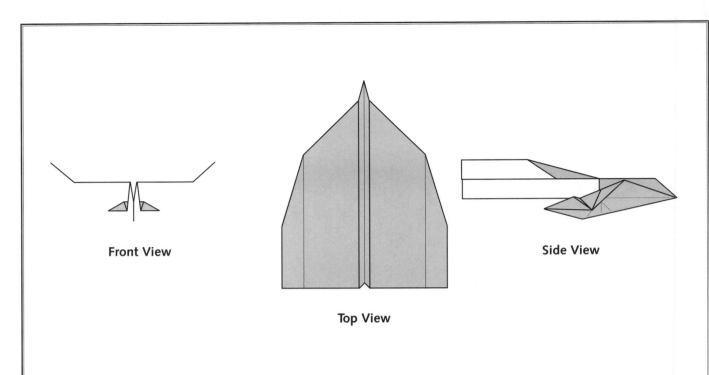

Front View

Top View

Side View

The bomb bays can carry a variety of ballistic objects. Pellets made from fissionable plutonium work best, though other materials can be substituted. Bombwielder should be adjusted so that it either loops or stalls out in mid-flight, as the bomb bays will empty when it goes upside-down in a loop . The airplane tends to roll out of a stall, dropping its payload on the hapless denizens below.

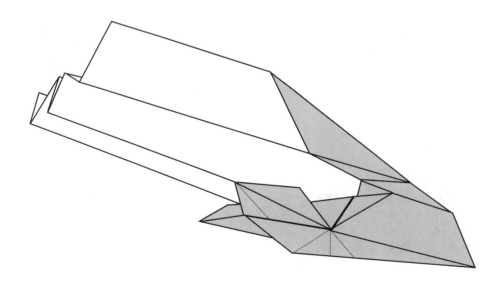

Bombwielder

Mark II-Air-to-Surface
Missile Launcher

By changing the war pod, Bombwielder can launch other airplanes while in flight. Begin with Step 21 of the Bombwielder.

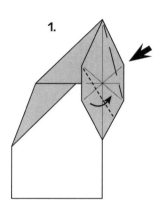

1.

On one side only, valley fold the rear of the war pod over as far as it will go. Also on one side only, sink the front of the warpod from corner to corner.

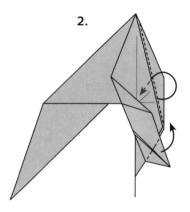

2.

Valley fold the lower front of the war pod and tuck it into the pocket formed in the previous step. Mountain fold the tip of the war pod flap around and behind its counterpart. Turn over.

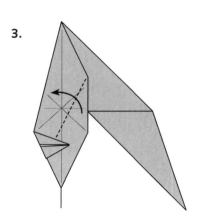

3.

Valley fold the war pod as in Step 1.

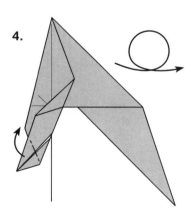

4.

Wrap this flap back around the war pod as in Step 2. Turn the model over.

5.

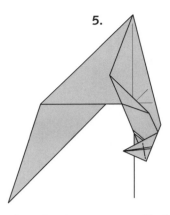

The explanation is more complicated than the fold. There is one loose flap that needs to be tucked in to lock down the war pod. Where this flap intersects the layer just in front of it, make a mountain fold.

6.

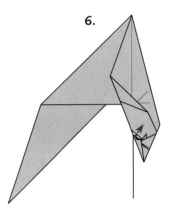

Now tuck the little bit of this flap sticking out under the layer in front of it. Fold the wings and stabilizers as shown previously.

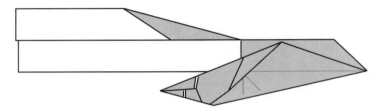

By inserting a small airplane into the slit that runs along the upper rear of the war pod, you can use the Bombwielder to launch missiles in flight. The plane serving as a missile must have a long sharp nose; Mach II is a good example. The missile should be made to quarter-scale, so you should start with a 2 ¼ × 1⅜ inch sheet of paper. If you stick the airplane far into the war pod it will be very tightly held, whereas if just barely inserted, it might separate from the bomber on takeoff. If adjusted just right, the airplane will be launched during high-speed turns, allowing the Bombwielder to launch an air-to-surface missile.

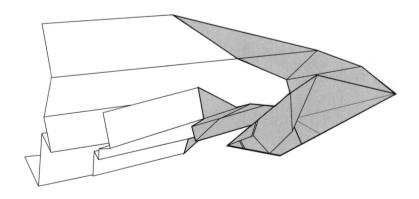

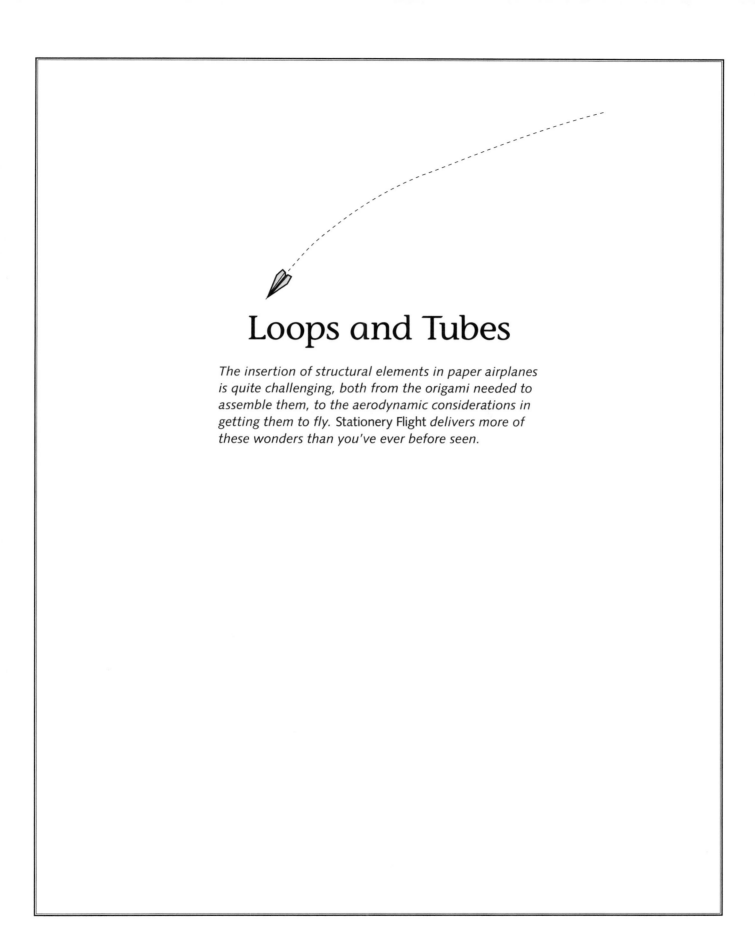

Loops and Tubes

The insertion of structural elements in paper airplanes is quite challenging, both from the origami needed to assemble them, to the aerodynamic considerations in getting them to fly. Stationery Flight *delivers more of these wonders than you've ever before seen.*

Phantom Cruiser

This Pagodor spinoff is a remarkably smooth glider. Launch with a slow, easy throw. Begin with Step 2 of the Pagodor Volant.

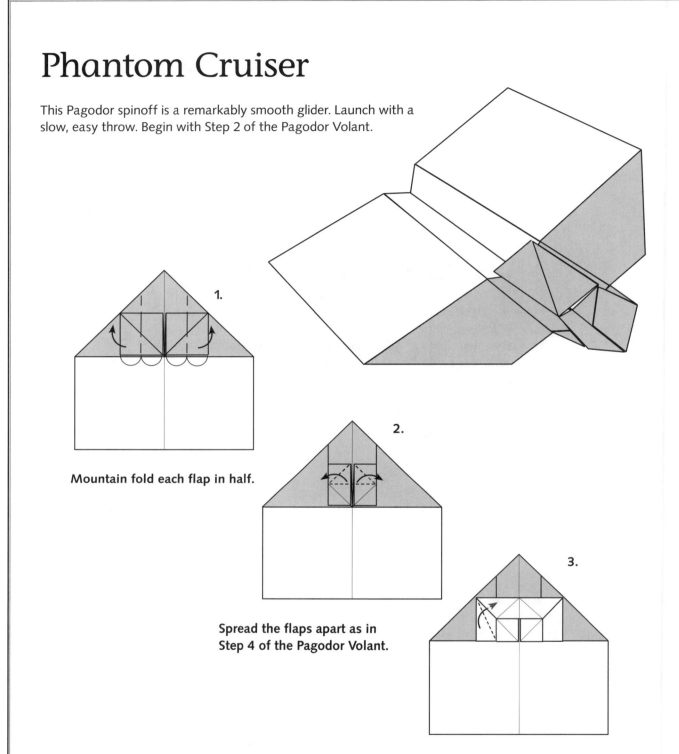

1.

Mountain fold each flap in half.

2.

Spread the flaps apart as in Step 4 of the Pagodor Volant.

3.

Valley fold one side only and tuck underneath.

4.

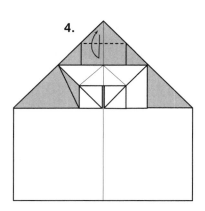

Valley fold and crease the top well.
Unfold.

5.

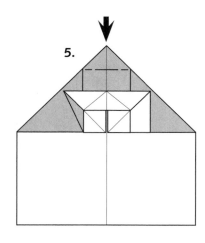

Sink along the crease made
in the previous step.

6.

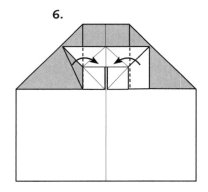

Valley fold the top flaps only
as far as they will go.

7.

Valley fold and open out as in
Step 5 of the Pocket Aerobat.

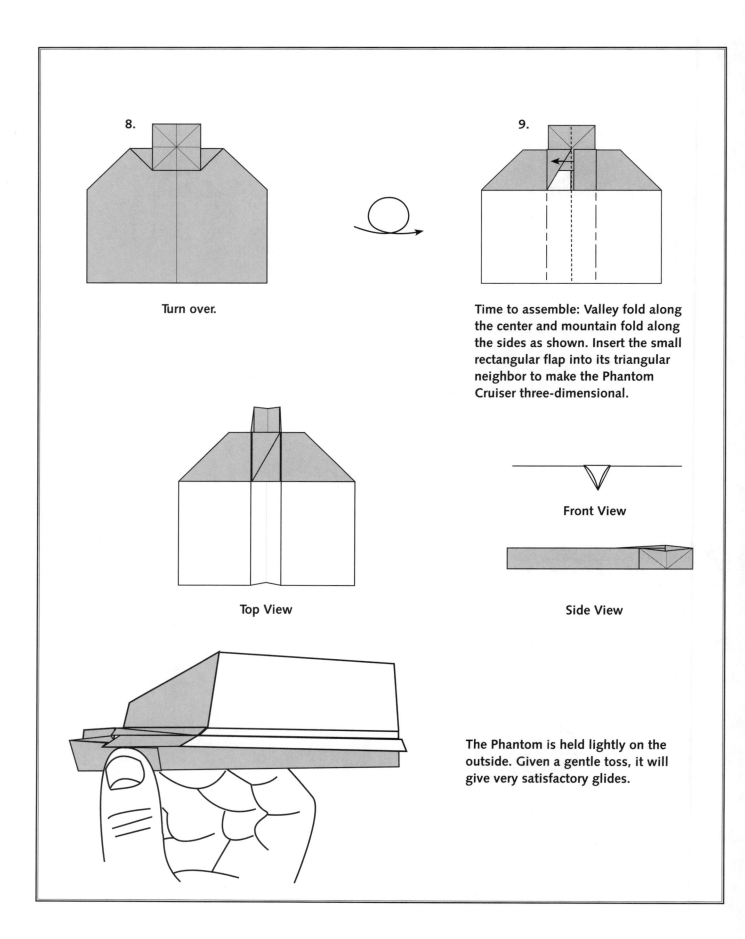

8.

Turn over.

9.

Time to assemble: Valley fold along the center and mountain fold along the sides as shown. Insert the small rectangular flap into its triangular neighbor to make the Phantom Cruiser three-dimensional.

Top View

Front View

Side View

The Phantom is held lightly on the outside. Given a gentle toss, it will give very satisfactory glides.

Starliner

This unusual design can be launched with force for stunning acrobatics, or it can be softly dropped for smooth glides. Begin with Step 5 of the Aerobotch.

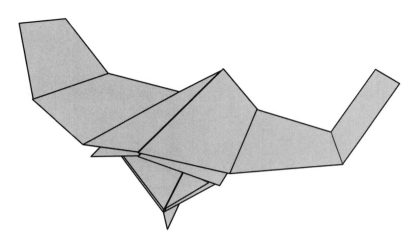

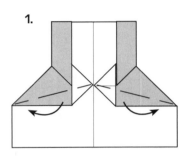

1.

Mountain fold the corners underneath.

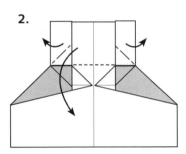

2.

Squash fold the upper flap downwards.

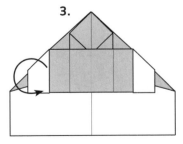

3.

Turn the outlying flap inside out on one side only.

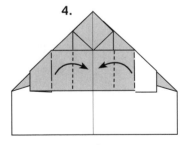

4.

Pleat the upper layer into the center.

5.

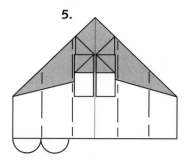

The outlying flaps of the top layer are sticking straight up. Mountain fold the wings and stabilizers as shown.

6.

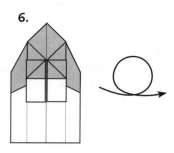

Turn so the model faces you to the side.

7.

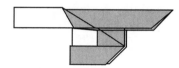

Side view: Slip one of the flaps hanging down into the other.

8.

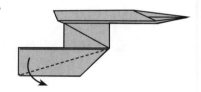

Enlargement: Valley fold the two flaps together as far as they will go.

9.

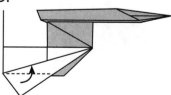

Narrow the flap with a valley fold.

10.

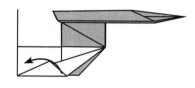

Mountain fold this flap inside to lock the two flaps together.

11.

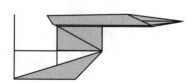

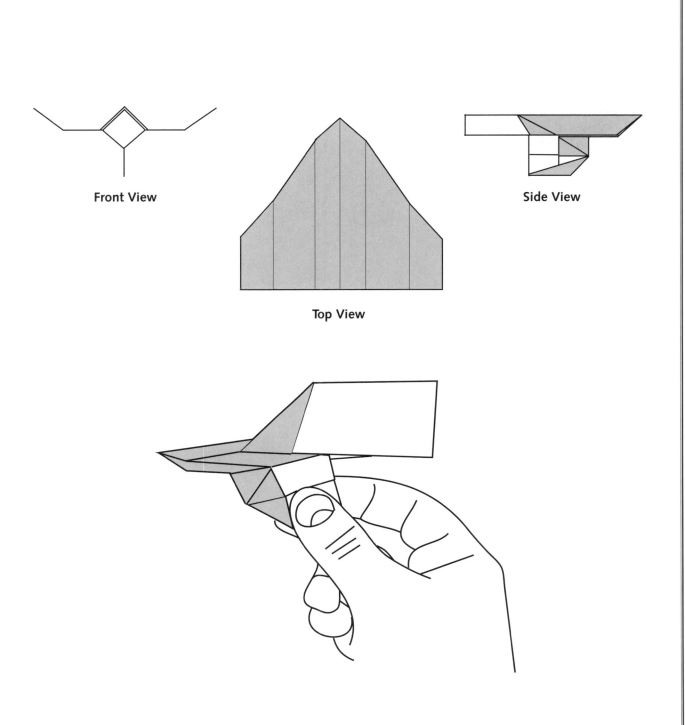

Front View

Top View

Side View

Starliner can be held by the lower vertical stabilizer for launch.
Thrown with soft force the airplane will make a satisfying glide, while
a more forceful throw will make for a wild ride.

95

Predator

This shark-like airplane starts with an 8 ½ × 5 ½ inch piece of paper folded in half width-wise and creased in the middle lengthwise.

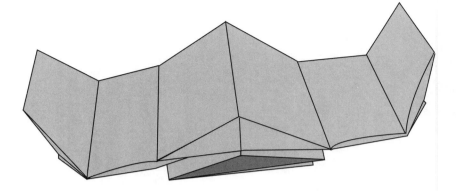

1.

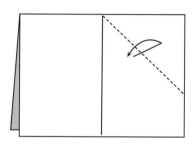

Fold so the folded edge lies at the center; crease lightly.

2.

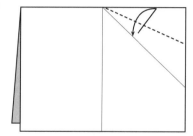

Fold so the folded edge lies on the crease made in Step 1; again crease lightly.

3.

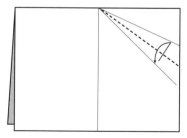

Fold so the two creases lie atop each other, then unfold.

4.

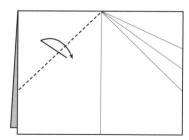

Use the crease from Step 4 to mark off an identical fold on the other side; unfold.

5.

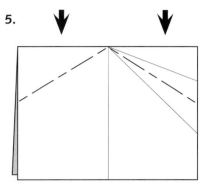

Reverse fold along the crease made in Steps 3 and 4.

6.

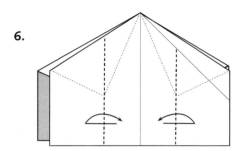

Valley fold the top layer only as far as it will go.

7.

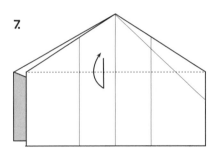

Valley fold the top upward and crease. Unfold.

8.

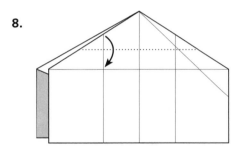

Valley fold so the double folded edge touches the intersection of the creases formed in Steps 7 and 8.

9.

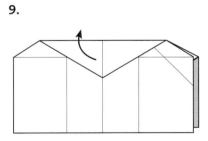

Unfold to Step 8.

10.

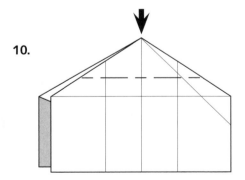

Sink along the crease formed in Step 9.

11.

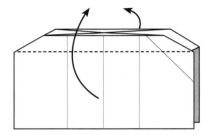

Valley fold up in front and behind.

12.

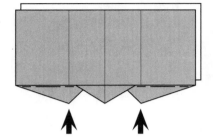

Reverse fold the two flaps into the body.

13.

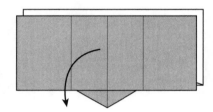

Unfold the upper flap.

14.

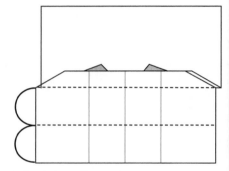

Fold the lower flap in half and then back up again.

15.

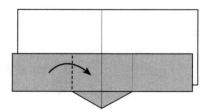

Valley fold one flap over.

16.

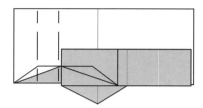

Crease the wing with mountain folds.

17.

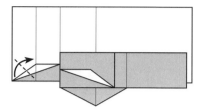

Reverse fold so the corner touches the crease made in Step

18.

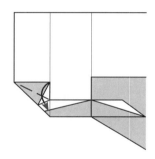

Valley fold the corner down and tuck it into the adjacent pocket.

19.

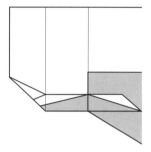

Repeat Steps 16 –19 on the other side.

20.

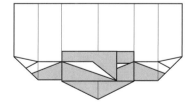

The two rectangular projections are hollow struts. Slide one all the way into the other. This will make the airplane triangular. At the same time, lift the wings and position the stabilizers.

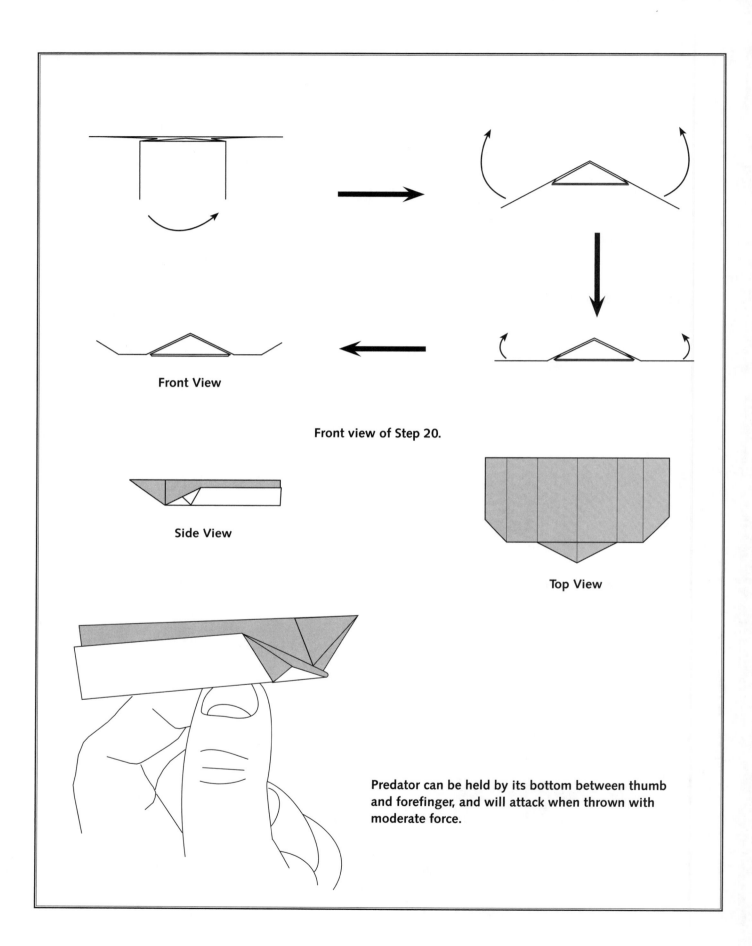

Front View

Front view of Step 20.

Side View

Top View

Predator can be held by its bottom between thumb and forefinger, and will attack when thrown with moderate force.

Ramjet

Another triangular airplane design that begins with a sheet of paper creased in half lengthwise and folded in half width-wise.

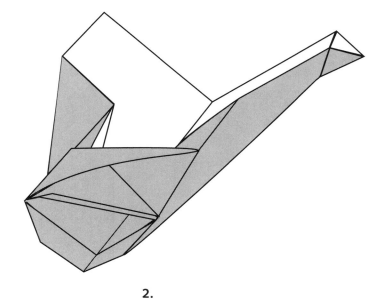

1.

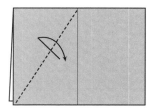

Valley fold from top center to bottom corner. Crease lightly.

2.

Valley fold so the top corner rests on the center, again creasing lightly.

3.

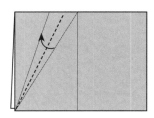

Valley fold so the two creases line up.

4.

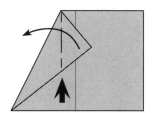

Squash fold.

5.

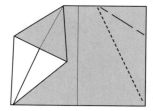

Repeat Steps 2 – 4
on the other side.

6.

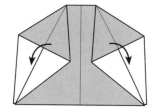

Fold the half-diamonds
underneath the top layer.

7.

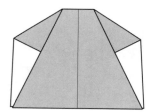

Turn the model over.

8.

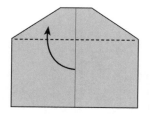

Valley fold the top layer
upwards.

9.

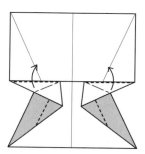

Squash fold the
protruding flaps
upward. Start the
top of the fold at the
crease indicated.

10.

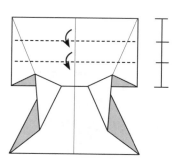

Valley fold the upper
rectangle in thirds.

11.

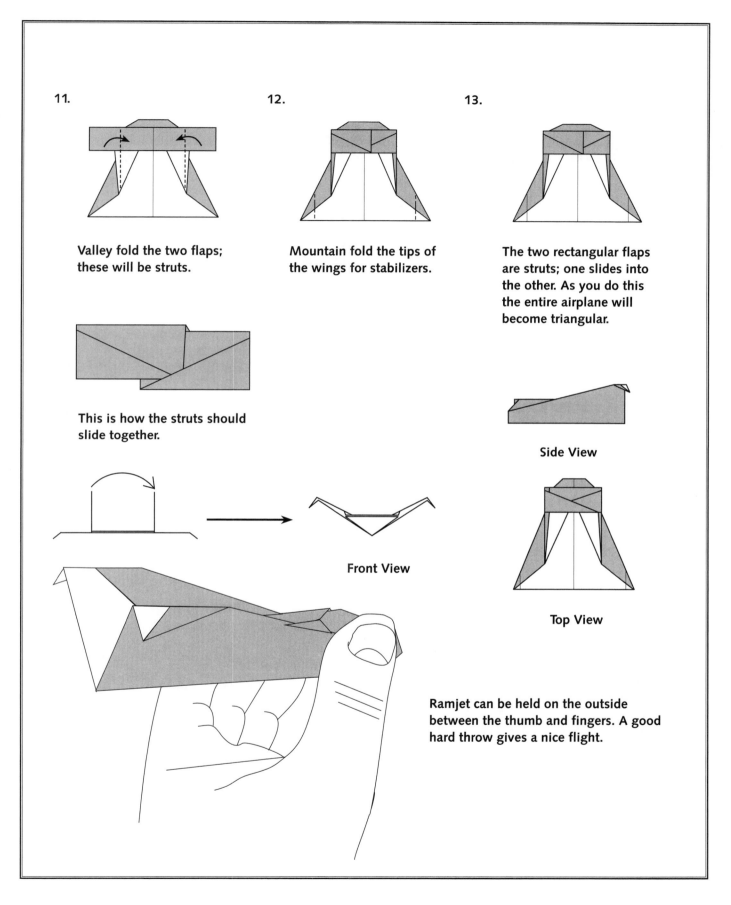

Valley fold the two flaps; these will be struts.

12.

Mountain fold the tips of the wings for stabilizers.

13.

The two rectangular flaps are struts; one slides into the other. As you do this the entire airplane will become triangular.

This is how the struts should slide together.

Side View

Front View

Top View

Ramjet can be held on the outside between the thumb and fingers. A good hard throw gives a nice flight.

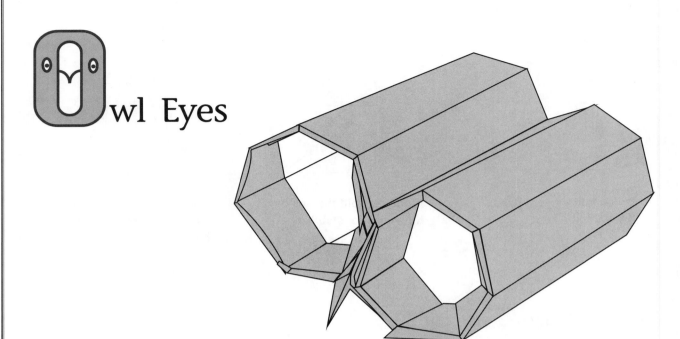

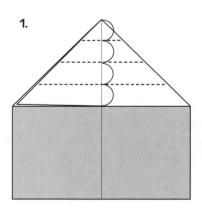

Owl Eyes

There's a traditional airplane that is one big tube. I always wanted to make a plane that had two tubes; what I got looks like an owl. What can I say? Start with the Canard Base, but start with the colored side of the paper facing up.

1.

Crease the upper triangle into fourths.

2.

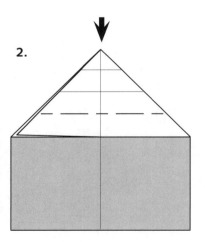

Sink along the first of the creases.

3.

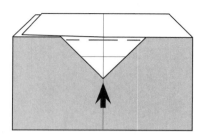

Sink upward along the next crease.

4.

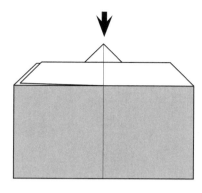

Sink downward one last time.

5.

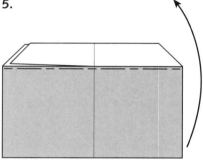

Mountain fold the single ply flap upward.

6.

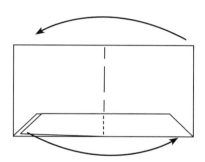

Mountain fold the large flap to the left and valley fold the small flap to the right.

7.

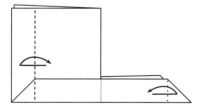

Make the valley folds shown, then unfold. Repeat behind.

8.

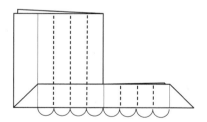

Valley fold into fourths the two areas between the creases made in Step 7 and the middle. Unfold.

9.

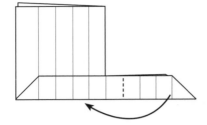

Valley fold the small flaps over along the crease nearest the middle.

10.

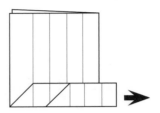

Pull out one layer and squash fold the rear as in Step 12 of the Multi-Stage Craft.

11.

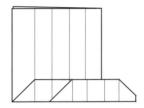

The result: Steps 12 and 13 show how to lock the front together.

12.

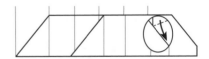

Cutaway view: Fold the middle layer over as far as it will go.

13.

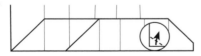

Make a similar fold on the other side.

14.

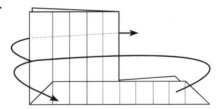

Assembly time: The thin flaps at the right fit between the two layers of the thicker flaps. The thin flap should go in all the way to the crease nearest the middle; that's the fold used in Step 10. The easiest way to do this is to wrap the two flaps around and station the thin one just behind the thick part where it will insert. Line up the creases, then slide the thin flap forward and between. You should end up with a binocular shape.

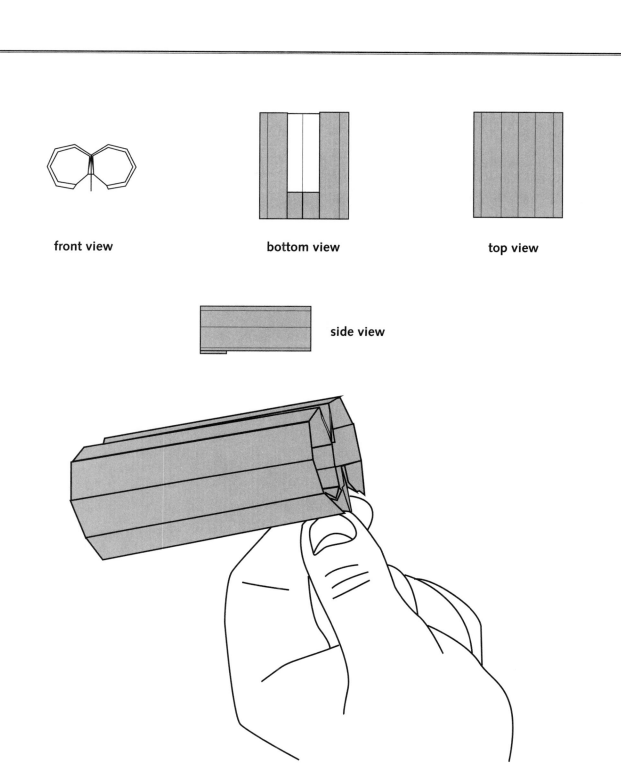

front view

bottom view

top view

side view

Owl Eyes can be launched using the little tab that sticks out below the tubes. Throw it hard; it will give a nice flight, and attract lots of attention with its unusual lines.

Loopstar

This was the first of my efforts to incorporate a loop or tube into an airplane. It still remains one of my favorites. Begin with the Airplane Base.

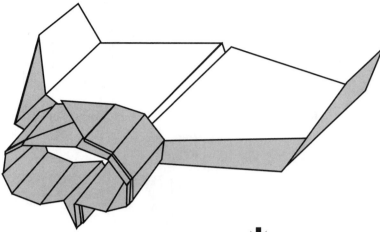

1.

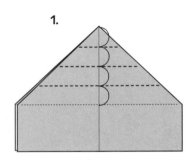

Divide the upper triangle into fourths. Crease well and unfold.

2.

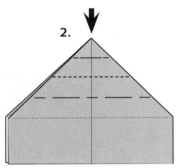

Sink up and down along the creases as in Steps 2–5 of the Owl Eyes.

3.

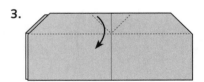

Valley fold one layer only. The innermost sink will open out.

4.

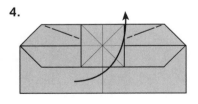

Swivel the lower flap up, squash folding the resulting pocket.

5.

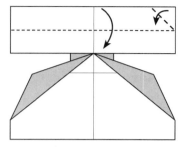

Fold one corner in, then valley fold the upper section in half.

6.

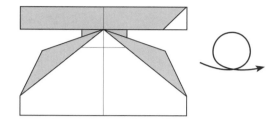

Turn the model over.

7.

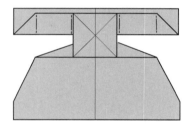

Make the mountain folds shown and unfold.

8.

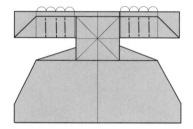

Crease the paper in that's between the Step 7 creases into fourths.

9.

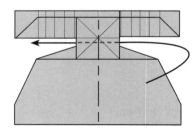

Mountain fold in half.

10.

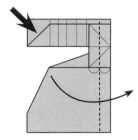

Valley fold the wings down by dividing the rectangular base in half as shown.

11.

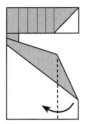

Fold up the stabilizers.

12.

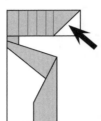

Time for the final assembly. The long narrow flaps in front form Loopstar's loop. The ends should fit together, a corner goes into a pocket (marked with an arrow in Step 10) on the upper side, while a different corner goes into the pocket shown here on the underside. The ends should slide into each other up to the most outlying creases.

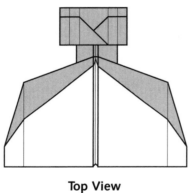

Top View

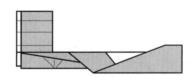

Side View

Front View

It's important to keep the wings downswept at an angle that puts them beneath the loop. This keeps turbulence generated by the loop off the wings and allows Loopstar to fly.

Thunder Jet

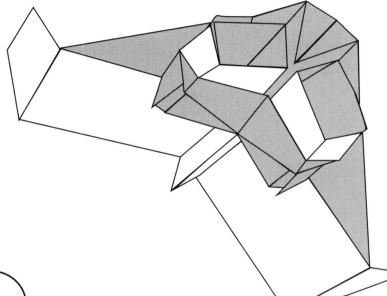

This jet includes nacelles. Begin
with a sheet of paper creased in
half lengthwise.

1.

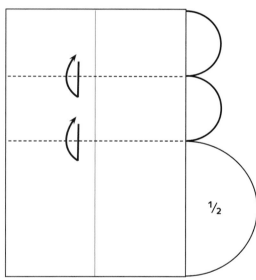

Creasing lightly, valley fold in half
width-wise and then in half again.

2.

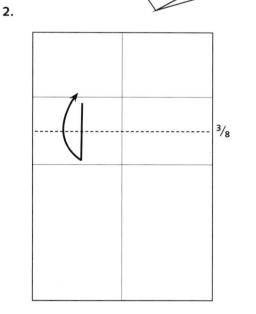

Valley fold so that the two creases line
up. Crease lightly, then unfold.

3.

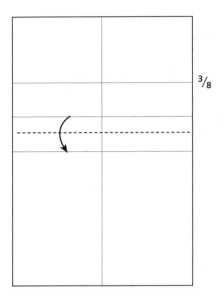

$^3/_8$

One more time. Valley fold so that the 3/8 crease you made in the previous step lies flush with the midline.

4.

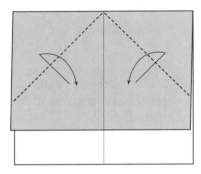

Valley fold the top corners to the center and unfold.

5.

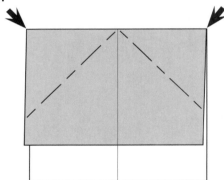

Reverse fold the corners inward.

6.

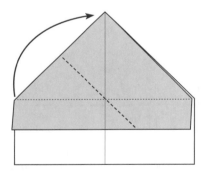

Valley fold so the corner of the triangle (whose bottom side is hidden from view) meets the point on top.

7.

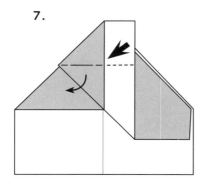

Squash fold.

8.

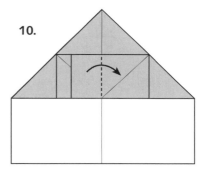

Valley fold the rectangular flap where it crosses the center line. At the same time, valley fold as in Step 6 and flatten the resulting pocket.

9.

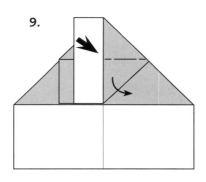

Squash fold as in Step 7.

10.

Valley fold the uppermost rectangular portion (four layers) where it crosses the center line.

11.

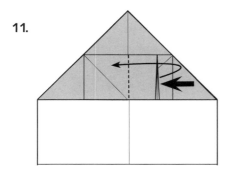

Fold two layers over to the right. A pocket will form between the second and third layers. When this is squash folded the open end of the squash will face upward.

12.

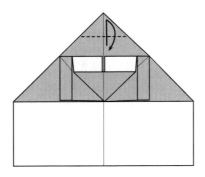

The result: Fold the top point halfway down, crease well, and unfold.

13.

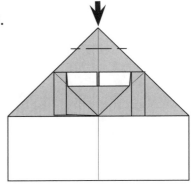

Sink the top along the crease made in the previous step.

14.

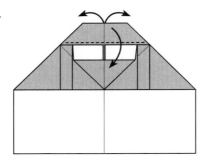

Valley fold the top layer down while spreading out the sink.

15.

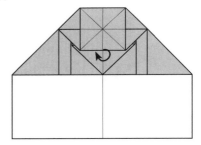

Tuck the lower part of the spread sink underneath the other layers.

16.

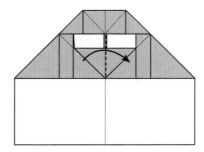

Valley fold the top layer over.

17.

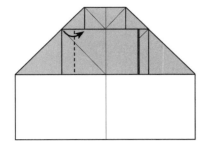

Valley fold the left hand flap so that its edge meets the intersection of two layers.

18.

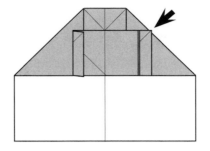

Repeat Steps 16 and 17 on the other side.

19.

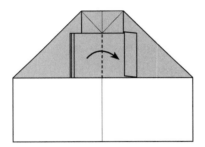

Fold one layer over to the right.

20.

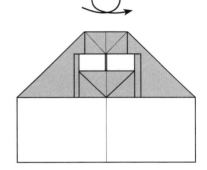

Turn the model over.

21.

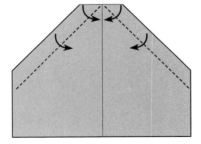

Valley fold so that the front edges line up with the centerline. Be careful to keep the folds symmetrical.

22.

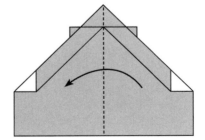

Valley fold in half.

23.

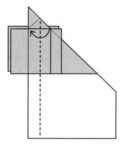

Valley fold the wings.

24.

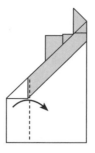

Valley fold the stabilizers.

25.

Now it's time to assemble the engine nacelles. Spread the wings out perpendicular to the fuselage. Raise the stabilizers perpendicular to the wings, and let the flaps folded over in Steps 16 and 17 drop down and lie perpendicular to the wings.

26.

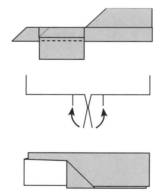

Valley fold the long flaps at their base. Fit their ends over those of the shorter flaps above to form the engines. A front view is shown for clarity. The bottom diagram illustrates how these two flaps should fit together.

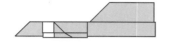

Side View

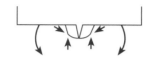

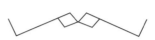

Front View

Pinch the corners of the engines to lock them into place. Bring the wings down into a downswept position and shape the engines into rectangles.

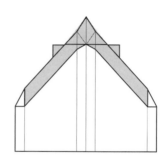

Top View

Unfortunately, Thunder Jet is tough to get to fly, but I've yet to make one that didn't work. Start by turning the rear margins of the wings up. This should make the plane fly while veering to one side. On the side opposite the direction in which it turns you need to make a rudder; bend the rear edge of the vertical stabilizer outward. This should cause the plane to fly a straight course.

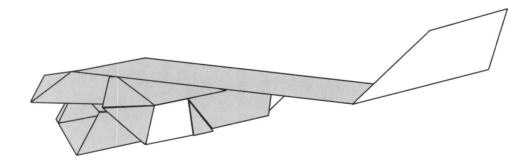

Two-Piece Models

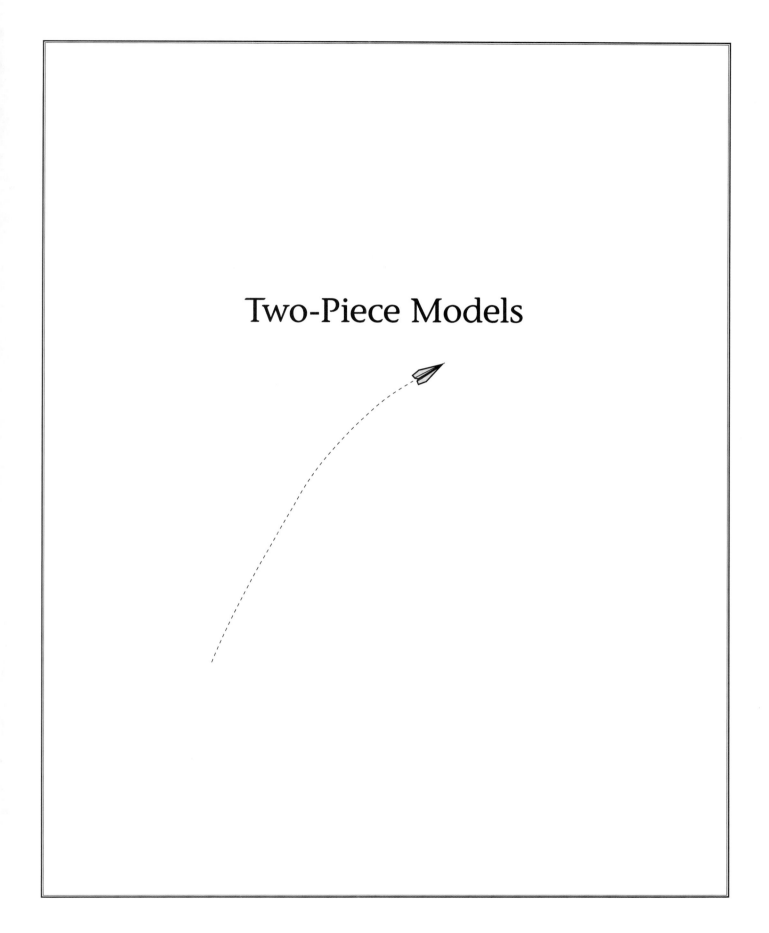

Gemini

Start with an 8½ x 5½ inch sheet of paper creased down the middle.

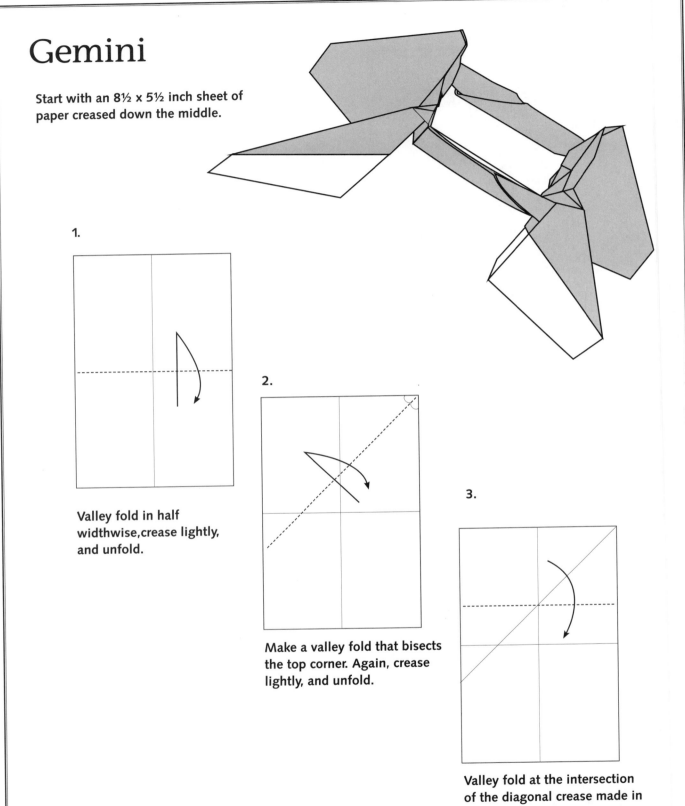

1.

Valley fold in half widthwise, crease lightly, and unfold.

2.

Make a valley fold that bisects the top corner. Again, crease lightly, and unfold.

3.

Valley fold at the intersection of the diagonal crease made in Step 2 and the center line.

4.

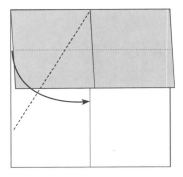

Valley fold so the crease made in Step 1 lies on the center line.

5.

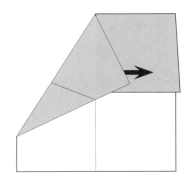

Pull out the underlying layer and flatten.

6.

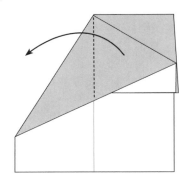

Valley fold the top flap over across the center.

7.

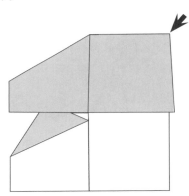

Repeat Steps 4-6 on the other side.

8.

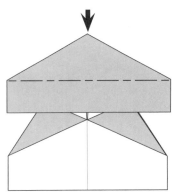

Sink the top.

9.

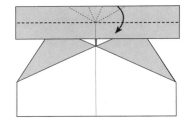

Valley fold the resultant rectangle in half, flattening two pockets as you do so.

10.

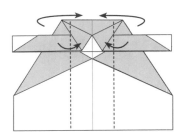

Valley fold the struts toward you and the fins facing away from you.

11.

Now go back to the beginning and repeat Steps 1-10 on a second piece of paper (two piece design, remember?). You will then be able to interlock the two halves using the struts.

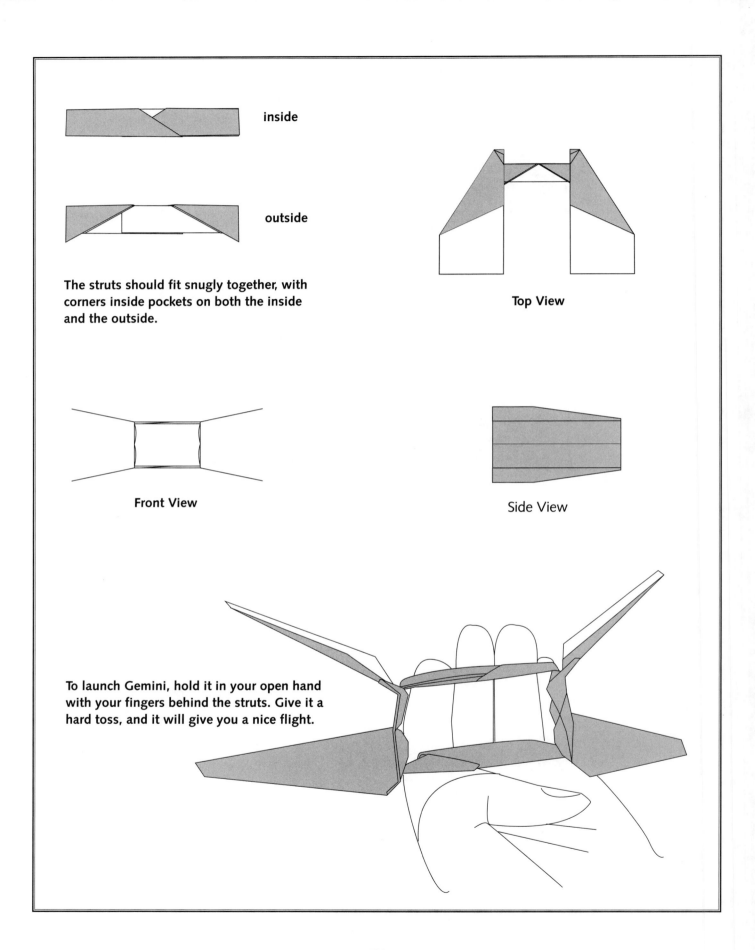

inside

outside

The struts should fit snugly together, with corners inside pockets on both the inside and the outside.

Top View

Front View

Side View

To launch Gemini, hold it in your open hand with your fingers behind the struts. Give it a hard toss, and it will give you a nice flight.

Jet Fighter

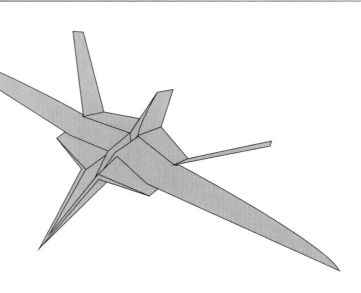

Begin the fuselage and empennage of this two-piece wonder by folding the Multi-Stage Craft up to Step 6.

1.

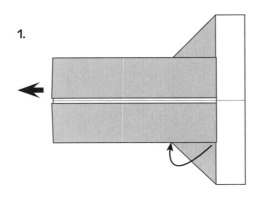

You have a rectangular flap partially covering a trapezoidal area. Pull the rectangle to the left. The folded edge at its rear will flatten out, leaving a crease that will be your guide. Line up this crease with the forward edge of the trapezoid.

2.

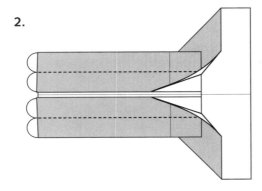

Flatten the resulting upheaval by valley folding the long flaps in half. Give all the folds a sharp crease, and make certain the flaps in back (the rear wings) are lined up straight.

3.

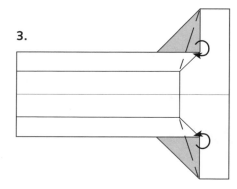

Mountain fold the rearward corners underneath.

4.

Mountain fold the fuselage in half.

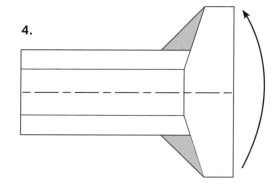

5.

Crease an angle bisector in the front, and then unfold.

Valley fold so that the crease made in the previous step lines up with the bottom. Unfold.

6.

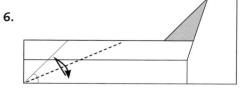

7.

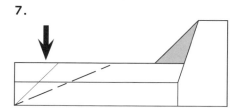

Reverse fold the front along the crease made in Step 6.

8.

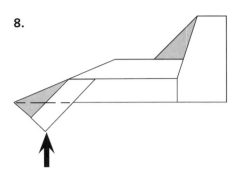

Reverse fold back up along the crease made in Step 5.

9.

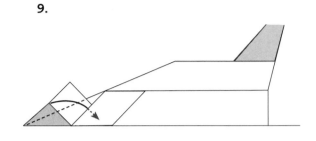

Valley fold the remaining portion downward and tuck the corner into the adjacent pocket.

10.

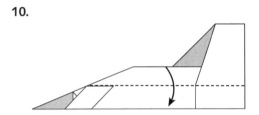

Valley fold the rear wings and sides downward.

11.

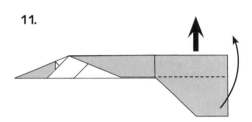

Valley fold the rear wings up and pull out a tail as in Step 12 of the Multi-Stage Craft.

12.

The fuselage and empennage are completed.

Jet Fighter – wings

Once again you will need an 8½ x 5½ inch sheet of refined cellulose (that's paper to you non-scientist) folded down the middle.

1.

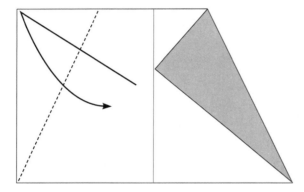

Valley fold from the bottom corner to the top edge. The top corner should rest on the center line, as shown on the right. Crease very lightly, and unfold.

2.

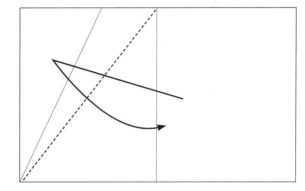

Valley fold from the bottom corner to the top edge center. Again, crease with a light touch and unfold.

3.

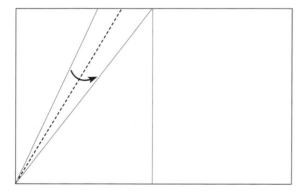

Valley fold so the creases made in the previous two steps line up.

4.

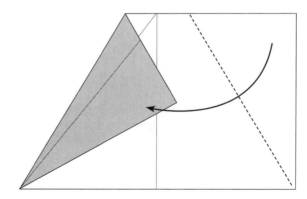

Repeat Steps 1-4 on the other side.

5.

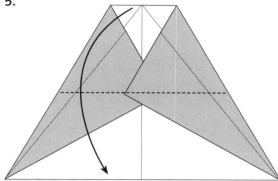

Valley fold across so the top edge meets the bottom edge.

6.

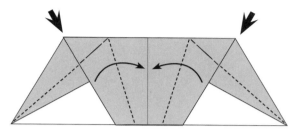

Valley fold the top layer so the folded edge on the outside lines up with the center line. Pockets will form at the top. Squash fold these, running the folds down to the outside corners.

7.

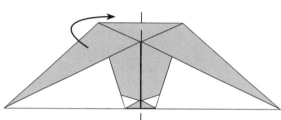

Mountain fold the wings in half.

To assemble, slide the wings into the cleft in the fuselage. Valley fold the wings where they meet the body of the aircraft.

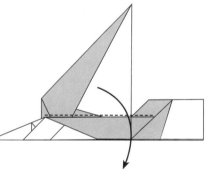

Pull the wings and their supports out perpendicular to the body of the airplane. The rear wings will point out and off to an angle.

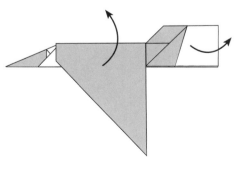

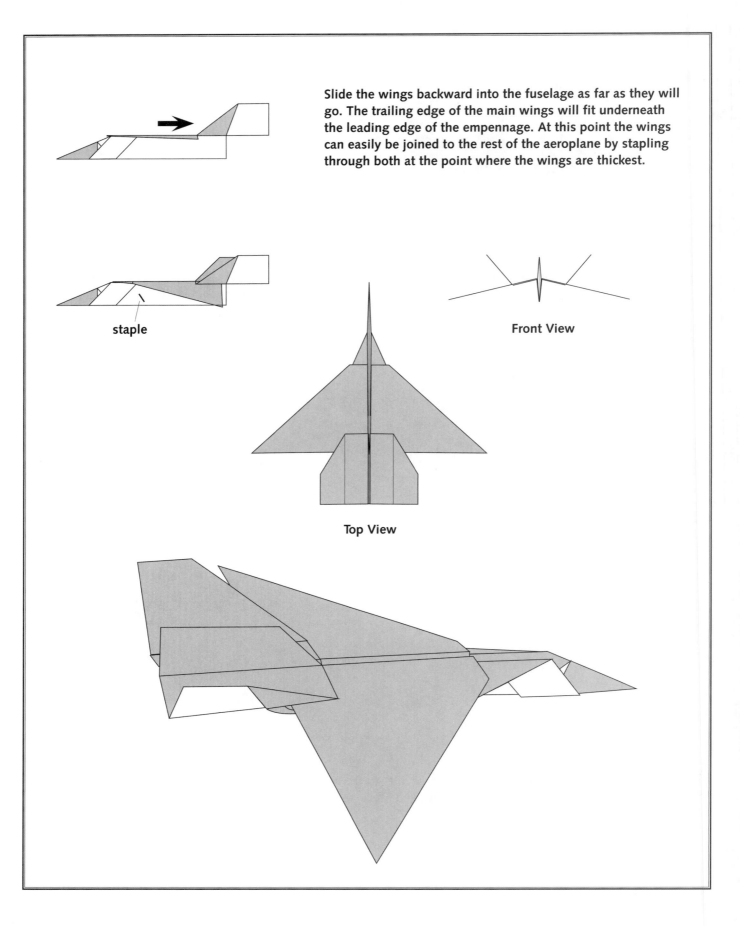

Slide the wings backward into the fuselage as far as they will go. The trailing edge of the main wings will fit underneath the leading edge of the empennage. At this point the wings can easily be joined to the rest of the aeroplane by stapling through both at the point where the wings are thickest.

staple

Front View

Top View

Biplane

Here it is, three years in the making, my biplane. Use 2 sheets of 8½ x 11 inch paper (that's right, the stuff you've been cutting in half all along you don't have to cut), and a metallic portrait of the sixteenth president.

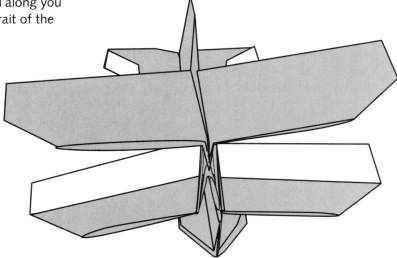

1.

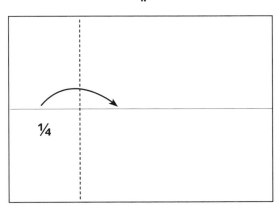

Valley fold the paper one quarter of the way in.

2.

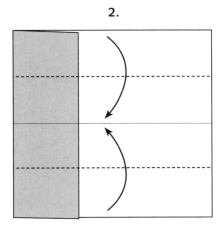

Valley fold both sides into the center.

3.

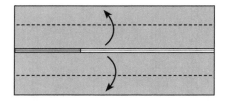

Valley fold back out to the edge.

4.

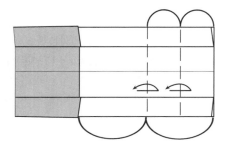

Crease lightly as shown.

5.

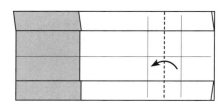

Valley fold so that the two creases line up.

6.

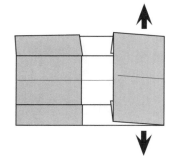

Pull out and squash fold the layers hidden under the top flap.

7.

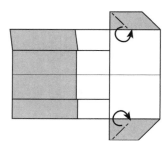

Mountain fold the corners underneath, then turn over.

8.

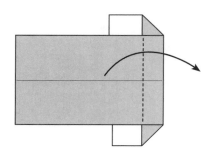

Valley fold the long flap over as far as it will go.

9.

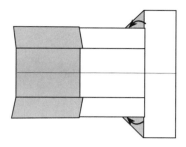

Shift the long flap forward as in Step 1 of the Jet Fighter.

10.

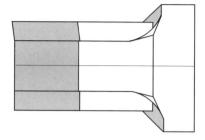

Flatten the resulting pockets. No landmarks here, just use your best judgment.

11.

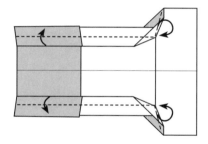

Mountain fold the rear of the flap squash folded in the previous step. Valley fold the flaps at the sides in half.

12.

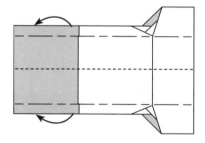

Mountain fold the outlying areas behind, then valley fold the model in half.

13.

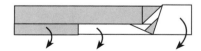

Pull down the top layers.

14.

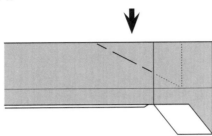

Sink the area shown. There's a layer of paper underneath the rightmost section; the sink fold should extend to the lower corner of this layer. Some paper will get pulled out in the process.

15.

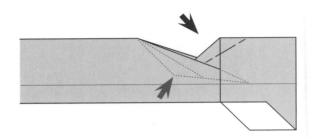

Sink to form the tail. The sink will continue into the fuselage and should make the tail the same length as the rear wings. Note that a countersink will be needed on the inside of the fuselage.

16.

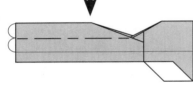

Sink once more to narrow the fuselage.

17.

Valley fold the rear wings and their supports up perpendicular to the fuselage.

18.

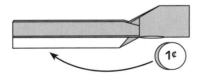

Insert a penny into the front. It should be held in place between the layer folded in Step 1 and the rest.

19.

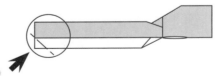

The next series of steps is designed to lock the front end together. Start by reverse folding the bottom flap in on one side only.

20.

Valley fold the inside layer over to lock the top together.

21.

View from the top. Crease the side flap along its angle bisector, then crease into fourths.

22.

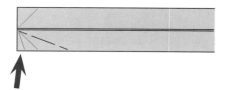

Reverse fold along the innermost crease.

23.

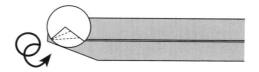

Part of this is a cutaway view. Roll the reverse folded flap inside along previously made creases. Repeat on the other side.

24.

Side view again. On the bottom, tuck the flap from one side into the pocket created in Step 20. Round off the top a little with a reverse fold.

Biplane – wings

Another 8½ × 5½ inch sheet of paper creased down the middle is required.

1.

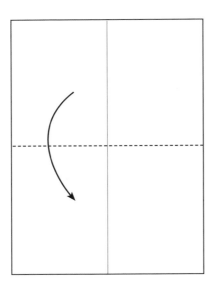

Fold in half width-wise.

2.

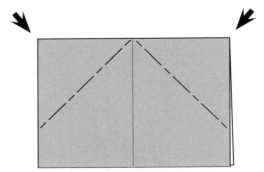

Reverse fold the corners inward.

3.

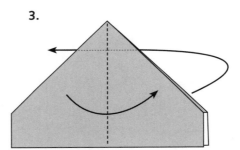

Valley fold one flap to the right in front and mountain fold one flap to the left behind.

4.

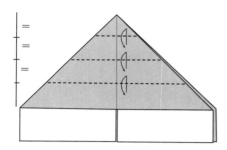

Crease the upper triangle into fourths.

5.

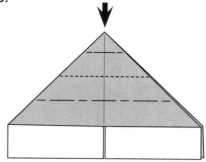

Sink up and down as in Loopstar and Owl Eyes.

6.

Fit the wings onto the fuselage.

7.

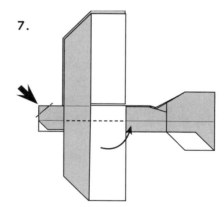

Valley fold the lower wings upward along the crease made in Step 17 of the fuselage. Reverse fold the front.

8.

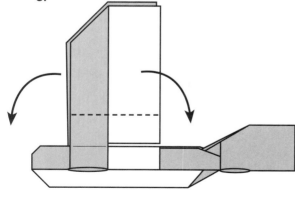

Fold the upper wings outward to match the lower wings.

9.

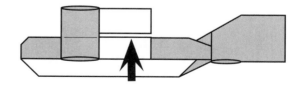

Sink the paper left over from Step 8 upward.

10.

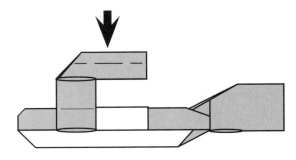

Squash fold the upper flap so that it lies
flat along the wings. Rotate the plane so
the top of the wings face you.

11.

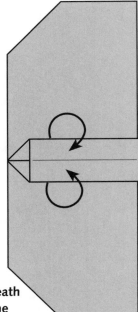

Sink the two resulting flaps underneath
the top layer of the wings. Rotate the
model so that its side faces you.

12.

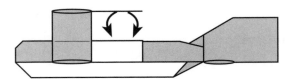

Then fold these two flaps down so they
rest perpendicular to the wings.

13.

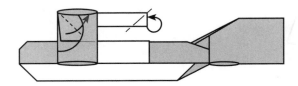

Finally, mountain fold the rear portions
of these flaps to the center to lock them
in place. Fold over a flap inside the front
of the wings to lock them together.

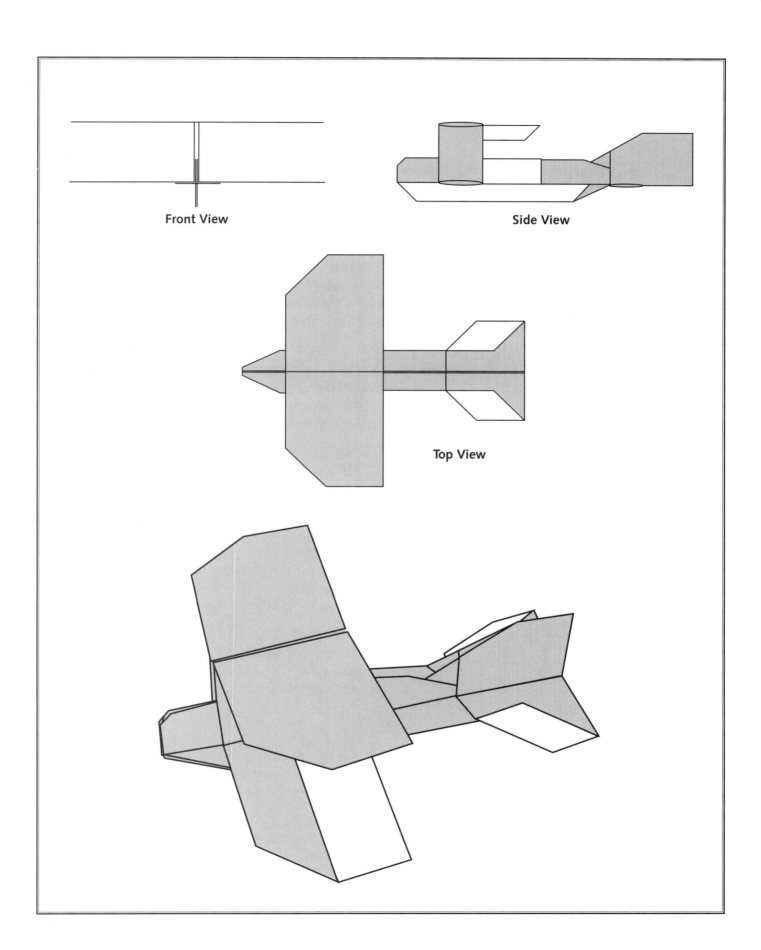

Front View

Side View

Top View

BIBLIOGRAPHY

The following list of origami books, covering both general subjects and airplanes, are recommended as being comprehensive, well-presented, creative and best of all, available via the usual avenues of book acquisition. The key letters after each title indicate the subject matter (**G** = General, **A** = Airplane) and level of complexity throughout each book (**B** = Beginner, **I** = Intermediate, **C** = Complex).

Araki, Chiyo
Origami for Christmas, Kodansha International, 1983/87 (**G, B, I**)

Biddle, Steve, Megumi Biddle
Essential Origami, St. Martin's Press, 1991 (**G, B, I**)

Biddle, Steve, Megumi Biddle
The New Origami, St. Martin's Press, 1993 (**G, B, I**)

Boursin, Didier
Advanced Origami: More than 60 Fascinating and Challenging Projects for the Serious Folder, Firefly Books Ltd., 2000 (**G, C**)

Boursin, Didier
Origami Airplanes, Firefly Books Ltd., 2001 (**A**)

Boursin, Didier
Origami Paper Animals, Firefly Books Ltd., 2001 (**G, I, C**)

Brill, David
Brilliant Origami, Japan Publications, 1996 (**G, I, C**)

Collins, John M.
The Gliding Flight: 20 Excellent Fold & Fly Paper Airplanes, Ten Speed Press (**A, B, I**)

Engel, Peter
Folding the Universe: Origami from Angelfish to Zen, Dover, 1994 (**G, I, C**)

Fuse, Tomoko
Unit Origami: Multidimensional Transformations Japan Publications, 1990 (**G, B, I, C**)

Fuse, Tomoko
Origami Boxes, Japan Publications, 1989 (**G, B, I**)

Gray, Alice, Kunihiko Kasahara
Magic of Origami, Japan Publications, 1985 (**G, B, I**)

Gross, Gay M.
Folding Napkins, Friedman Publishing Group, 1997 (**G, B, I**)

Honda, Isao
World of Origami, Japan Pub. Trading Co., 1965/76 (**G, B, I, C**)

Hsu, Gery
How to Make Origami Airplanes That Fly, Dover Publications (**A, B, I**)

Hull, Thomas & Robert E. Neale
Origami Plain and Simple, St. Martin's Press, 1994 (**G, B, I**)

Hull, Thomas & Sergei Afonkin
Russian Origami, St. Martin's Press, 1998
(**G, B, I, C**)

Kasahara, Kunihiko
Origami Made Easy, Japan Publications, 1973/88
(**G, B, I**)

Kasahara, Kunihiko
Origami for the Connoisseur, Japan Publications, 1998, Japanese (**G, B, I, C**)

Kasahara, Kunihiko
Amazing Origami, Sterling, 2001
(**G, B, I, C**)

Kasahara, Kunihiko
Origami Omnibus, Japan Publications (**G, B, I, C**)

Kitamura, Keiji
Origami Treasure Chest, Japan Publications, 1991
(**G, B, I**)

Lang, Robert J.
Complete Book of Origami,Dover, 1988 (**G, I, C**)

Lang, Robert J., & Stephen Weiss
Origami Zoo, St. Martin's Press, 1990 (**G, C**)

Lang, Robert
Origami In Action, St. Martin's Press, 1997 (**G, I, C**)

Montroll, John
Origami Inside Out (*2nd Ed.*), Dover, 1993 (**G, I, C**)

Montroll, John
Birds in Origami,Dover, 1995 (**G, I, C**)

Montroll, John
Origami for the Enthusiast, Dover, 1979/80 (**G, I, C**)

Montroll, John
Mythological Creatures and the Chinese Zodiac in Origami, Dover Publications, 1996 (**G, B, I, C**)

Montroll, John
Dollar Bill Animals in Origami, Dover Publications, 2000 (**G, B, I, C**)

Ow, Frances
Origami Hearts, Japan Publications, 1995 (**G, B, I**)

Palacios, Vicente
Fascinating Origami: 101 Models by Alfredo Cerceda, Dover, 1996 (**G, B, I**)

Palacios, Vicente
Origami for Beginners, Dover, 1999 (**G, B, I**)

Pang, Andrew
Star Trek: Paper Universe, Pocket Books, 2000
(**G, A, B, I, C**)

Pavarin, Franco & Luciano Spaggiari
Fold & Fly Paper Airplanes, Sterling Publishing, 1998
(**A, I, C**)

Temko, Florence & Richard Petersen *Paper Pandas and Jumping Frogs*, China Books & Periodicals, 1984
(**G, B, I**)

Temko, Florence
Origami for Beginners, Charles E. Tuttle Co., 1991
(**G, B**)

Temko, Florence
Origami Airplanes, Tuttle Publishing, 2003 (**A, B, I**)

Temko, Florence
Planes and Other Flying Things, Millbrook Press
(**A, B, I**)

Shafer, Jeremy
Origami to Astonish and Amuse, St. Martin's Press, Inc., 2001 (**G, I, C**)

Weiss, Stephen
Wings and Things: Origami that Flies, St. Martin's Press, 1984 (**A, B, I, C**)

Yamaguchi, Makoto
Kusudama: Ball Origami, Shufunotomo/Japan Publications, 1990 (**G, B, I**)

Yang, Thay
Exotic Paper Airplanes Cypress House, 2000 (**A, B, I**)

Yang, Thay
Exquisite Interceptors, Cypress House, 1996 (**A, B, I**)